THE
BREATHLESS
ORGASM

ALSO BY JOHN MONEY

Hermaphroditism: An Inquiry into the Nature of a Human Paradox, 1952

The Psychologic Study of Man, 1957

A Standardized Road-Map Test of Direction Sense (with D. Alexander and H. T. Walker, Jr.), 1965.

Sex Errors of the Body: Dilemmas, Education and Counseling, 1968.

Man and Woman, Boy and Girl: The Differentiation and Dimorphism of Gender Identity from Conception to Maturity (with A. A. Ehrhardt), 1972

Sexual Signatures (with Patricia Tucker), 1975

Love and Love Sickness: The Science of Sex, Gender Difference, and Pairbonding, 1980

The Destroying Angel: Sex, Fitness, and Food in the Legacy of Degeneracy Theory, Graham Crackers, Kellogg's Corn Flakes, and American Health History, 1985

Lovemaps: Clinical Concepts of Sexual/Erotic Health and Pathology, Paraphilia, and Gender Transposition in Childhood, Adolescence, and Maturity, 1986

Venuses Penuses: Sexology, Sexosophy, and Exigency Theory, 1986

Gay, Straight, and In-Between: The Sexology of Erotic Orientation, 1988

Vandalized Lovemaps: Paraphilic Outcome of Seven Cases in Pediatric Sexology (with M. Lamacz), 1989

Sexology of Genes, Genitals, Hormones, and Gender: Selected Readings, 1991

EDITED BY JOHN MONEY

Reading Disability: Progress and Research Needs in Dyslexia, 1962

Sex Research: New Developments, 1965

The Disabled Reader: Education of the Dyslexic Child, 1966

Transsexualism and Sex Reassignment (with R. Green), 1969

Contemporary Sexual Behavior: Critical Issues in the 1970's (with J. Zubin), 1973

Developmental Human Behavior Genetics (with W. K. Schaie, E. Anderson, and G. McClearn), 1975

Handbook of Sexology, vols. 1-5 (with H. Musaph), 1977

Traumatic Abuse and Neglect of Children at Home (with G. Williams), 1980

Handbook of Human Sexuality (with B. B. Wolman), 1980

Handbook of Sexology, vol. 6 (with H. Musaph and J. M. A. Sitsen), 1988

Handbook of Sexology, vol. 7 (with H. Musaph and M. Perry), 1990

ALSO BY DAVID HINGSBURGER

Changing Inappropriate Sexual Behaviours (with D. Griffiths and V. Quinsey), 1989

I-Contact: Sexuality and People with Developmental Disabilities, 1990

i to I: Self Concept and People with Developmental Disabilities, 1990

OPTIONS: Strategic Behavioural Interventions (with D. Griffiths), 1991

Being Sexual: Self Education Books for People with Physical or Developmental Disabilities (written in English and Blissymbolics) (with S. Ludwig), 1991

THE BREATHLESS ORGASM

A LOVEMAP BIOGRAPHY OF ASPHYXIOPHILIA

JOHN MONEY

GORDON WAINWRIGHT

DAVID HINGSBURGER

PROMETHEUS BOOKS
BUFFALO, NEW YORK

ACKNOWLEDGMENTS

Nelson Cooper extends special thanks to Arthur C. Plautz, M.D., the first physician who understood his problem and who, on a weekly schedule, treated him with Depo-Provera. Thanks also to Dr. Margaret Lamacz and Dr. Charles Annecillo from Dr. Money's office for their understanding and support.

95 94 93 92 91   5 4 3 2 1

Library of Congress Cataloging-in-Publication Data

Money, John, 1921-
    The breathless orgasm : a lovemap biography of asphyxiophilia / John Money, Gordon Wainwright, David Hingsburger.
        p.   cm.
    ISBN 978-0-87975-664-2
    1. Cooper, Nelson—Mental health. 2. Autoerotic asphyxia—Patients—
United States—Biography. 3. Autoerotic asphyxia—Patients—Rehabilitation.
4. Psychotherapy. I. Wainwright, Gordon. II. Hingsburger, David, 1952-
III. Title.
RC560.A97M66   1991
616.85′83—dc20   90-26691
                                                                              CIP

Dedicated to Susan and Dennis Danielson,
and Carol and Gerald Dusick,
and to the memory of their sons,
William Danielson and
Bradley J. Dusick.

Contents

10   Contents

PART FOUR: COMMENTARY

Preface

There was a monster in Nelson Cooper's life. Only later did he discover that it had a name: "asphyxiophilia." For most of his youth, this monster was unspeakable. Nelson was literally incapable of speaking about it. The price of muteness was appeasement. To placate his unspeakable monster, Nelson obeyed its dictates. It compelled him like a living sacrifice to engage in a ritual of self-strangulation to achieve orgasm and thus to risk accidental autoerotic death. He didn't wish to die, but he never knew at which moment it would be too late to loosen the bonds of self-strangulation, and so to become another statistic in the catalog of autoerotic death.

Nelson Cooper escaped death so many times that he lived long enough to break the silence, to speak about his unspeakable self-sacrifice, and finally to find the way out of his torment. He is the only person who has ever written with the intensity of first-hand knowledge about what it is like to be an asphyxiophiliac. It was only after he had found how to break the wall of silence that the unspeakable became not only spoken but also written. He became possessed by the muse of autobiography in both verse and prose.

Though he would like to declare his triumph to the world in person, Nelson has opted for the safety of anonymity. This edited book is the outcome. It is a book the like of which has never before been written. It combines poetry, narrative, and commentary, drawing the reader into its erotic agony and ecstasy. It is the first autobiographic account by an asphyxiophiliac, or as Nelson sometimes refers to himself, "the asphyxiophiliac still living."

Tens of thousands of asphyxiophiliacs are not still living. Autoerotic death by self-asphyxiation is what the coroner reports. Some families speak of it only as suicide to hide their shame of death while masturbating. Sexology cannot do the same. It dare not hide the truth and tell a scientific lie. Sexology has no place for the timid. Sexologists must be prepared every day to meet the dragons of sex no matter how fearsome they may be. Those who are being pursued by them have no one else to turn to, no one who will listen without panic, outrage, or passing judgment. They bring their dragons into the clinic, they make urgent phone calls, and they write letters of desperation. Nelson wrote a desperate and terrifying poem, a scream of impotent rage against those who had not paid attention to his being in the dragon's clutches.

The Scream

They tested my ears when I was in kindergarten
They gave me puzzles to do
They said that I was looking for attention
They said that I wanted others to do my school work for me
They said that I was spoiled
They said that I was educable-retarded
They said that I was emotionally disturbed
They said that I could not go to college they said, said, said
They said that I had a below average IQ
They said that my learning skills were weak
They said that my study skills were poor
They said that my spelling was below average
They said that my reading comprehension was below average
They said that my listening skills were intact
They said that I play games
They said that I try to shock people
They said that I was a slender boy, somewhat small for my age
They said that I was uneducable
They said that I can't cope with the rest of the world
They said that I should go to a home for the mildly retarded
They said that school is too difficult for me
They gave me the MMPI*
They claimed that I had problems because of school
They claimed that I was born with the problems
They said that 50 percent was my mom's fault and 50 percent my own
They said that the school system was not at fault
They said that I was calling the hotlines to scare the nurses
They said that I was getting a sexual thrill out of telling the nurses
    my problems
THEY THEY THEY THEY THEY THEY THEY THEY THEY THEY
THEY THEY THEY THEY THEY THEY THEY THEY THEY THEY

---

*Minnesota Multiphasic Personality Inventory

THEY THEY THEY THEY THEY THEY THEY THEY THEY THEY
THEY THEY THEY THEY THEY THEY THEY THEY THEY THEY
THEY THEY THEY THEY THEY THEY THEY THEY THEY THEY
THEY THEY THEY THEY THEY THEY THEY THEY THEY THEY
THEY THEY THEY THEY THEY THEY THEY THEY THEY THEY
FUCK THEM FUCK THEM FUCK THEM FUCK THEM FUCK
FUCK THEM FUCK THEM FUCK THEM FUCK THEM FUCK
FUCK THEM FUCK THEM FUCK THEM FUCK THEM FUCK
I HATE THEM I HATE THEM I HATE THEM I HATE THEM I
I HATE THEM I HATE THEM I HATE THEM I HATE THEM I
FUCK THEM FUCK THEM FUCK THEM FUCK THEM FUCK
FUCK THEM FUCK THEM FUCK THEM FUCK THEM FUCK
FUCK THEM FUCK THEM FUCK THEM FUCK THEM FUCK
I HATE THEM I HATE THEM I HATE THEM I HATE THEM I
I HATE THEM I HATE THEM I HATE THEM I HATE THEM I
KILL
KILL
KILL
KILLLLLLLLLLLLLLLLLLLLLLLLLLLLLLLLLLLLLLLLLLLLL
The professionals are assholes they are assholes
They think they are experts they think they are gods
They destroy families
They destroy families
They are racists
They are racists
They railroad innocent people
They are assholes they are assholes
They destroy children with their tests
They destroy children with their tests
They label children with their tests
Anyone with a low IQ is considered crippled by professionals
They railroad the ones who have epilepsy
They label those who are picked on by other children
They destroy the ones who have Tourette's syndrome
They destroy the deaf
They destroy the blind
They destroy the retarded
They destroy those who don't have a chance
They destroy those with asthma
Who can't be sports stars
They destroy those with warts on their faces
Who are teased by others

Then that isn't enough
They try to destroy you again when you are grown up
They have destroyed me and I'm all ripped up inside
Well it's time for a revolution
Against this master race of professionals
We will label and destroy them
My mother was never given any correct professional instructions
On what to do with an educational problem child
Had she been told what to do she would have done it
The family doctor simply rules, and he says
It is a phase he's going through
Boy did I go through a lot of phases
I phased in and out all the time
Understanding television was easy
I simply turned up the volume

*   *   *

There was no doubt that something had to be done for Nelson!

Prologue

Currently, all long-term outcome studies in sexology have the value of scarcity. That justifies restoration of the tradition, widely accepted a century ago, of publishing long and thorough case studies. There is a special place in sexology at this present phase of its history for the detailed single case report, particularly the report of a unique case that has the paramount virtue of showing that accepted theory or dogma needs to be changed in order to accommodate a new hypothesis. That new hypothesis then leads to the devising of a research design whereby it may be tested.

This book is just such a case study. It is comprised of, for the most part, the actual autobiographical narrative and verse of Nelson Cooper, selected and edited from a much larger body of his writings.

It is an act of courageous public service for any person afflicted with a paraphilia, even one that is not sex offending, to expose the detailed data of his syndrome for the advancement of biomedical science and the improvement of public understanding; yet a scientific understanding of the origin and prevention of paraphilia is inevitably dependent on such detailed data. The great importance of this book is that there are factors in Nelson's developmental history that, though they do not provide a complete explanation of the origin of his particular paraphilic lovemap, do fit together to provide at least a partial explanation of its design.

Terminology

For the reader unfamiliar with sexology and its terminology, some definitions will be necessary to understand the following discussion and to gain insight into the condition that is described by the narrator of this sexual biography.

Asphyxiophilia is a sexual peculiarity in which sexuoerotic arousal and facilitation or attainment of orgasm are responsive to and dependent upon self-strangulation and asphyxiation up to, but not including, loss of consciousness. When the ritual is autoerotic, as in the case of Nelson, split-second failure to release the noose or gag at the onset of orgasm can result in death.

Asphyxiophilia is one of many *paraphilias,* the accepted medical term for what in legal terminology is called a perversion or deviancy, and in the vernacular is referred to as "kinky."

Paraphilias of all types result from the malformation of an individual's *lovemap,* a term coined to describe the developmental representation or template in the mind/brain which depicts the idealized lover and the acts that are desired in the idealized, romantic, erotic, and sexualized relationship. A lovemap exists in mental imagery first, in dreams and fantasies, and then may be translated into action with a partner or partners.

Under optimum conditions, prenatally and postnatally, a lovemap differentiates as heterosexual without complexities. Age-concordant, gender-different, sexuoerotic rehearsal play in infancy and childhood is prerequisite to healthy heterosexual lovemap formation. Deprivation and neglect of such play may induce pathology of lovemap formation, as also may prohibition, prevention, and abusive punishment and discipline. Conversely, exposure too abruptly to socially tabooed expressions of sexuoeroticism may traumatize lovemap formation. Although lovemap pathology has its genesis early in life, it manifests itself in full only after puberty.

Ignorance Is Not Bliss

Nelson's autobiographical memories, recounted in the following pages, illustrate the principle that a paraphilia has its onset early in childhood, before puberty; that it flourishes in the sexual vacuum created by being deprived of normal sexual learning and normal sexual rehearsal play; and that it is not "caught" from viewing or reading commercial pornography. Nelson was raised in a morally strict and religious household, and was educated in a Catholic parochial school. He was deprived of access to sexual knowledge in print because of misdiagnosed hearing and learning problems as a child. His hearing impairment and eccentric behavior deprived him also of sharing the sexual knowledge of his peer group. He was sixteen before he knew how a baby is made.

The desire to keep sexual information from children is still strong in this society, as it always has been. As a result, parents and even most professionals who work with children have never had any training in sexuality or sexual issues with children. The training that does exist for professionals is primarily in biology. There is no professional training in the sexology of childhood, and there is no pediatric sexology clinic anywhere in the nation. Neither is there an adolescent sexology clinic, nor even a department of sexology in any university school of medicine or basic science.

The following first-person narrative demonstates that Nelson continuously sought help but was neglected or, worse still, rejected. Things became no better as he became an adult. It is astounding to read of his attempts to gain access to service and assistance of any kind, only to be frustrated by platitudes and judgments of causality and personal responsibility. Telling a young man who clearly describes a serious sexual obsession to "just not think about it" would be funny if it were not so tragic. Telling a young man who is masturbating to fantasies of sexual death that imagination not put into practice is acceptable is malpractice.

The only formal sex education Nelson received was from a single, fundamentalist religious booklet supplied by his older brother that gave fake doctrine disguised as fact. He was unable to form a coherent understanding of his own sexuality from this booklet. Ignorance is not bliss. Nelson's ignorance was enforced, immoral, and dangerous. He did not receive clear, understandable and functional sex education until he began treatment as an adult. He classifies this sex education as part of his therapy. His desire for love and affection was very strong, yet he did not succeed even in making friends. He suffers from a still unidentified factor prerequisite to pairbonding and of having limerence—i.e., the experience of falling in love—requited. For him, love was always unrequited. What the future holds for love requited, though it cannot be prophesied, is not without hope.

Nelson suffered many deprivations and abuses not only from the family, church, and school system under which he was reared but also from the medical/psychiatric establishment. The ultimate indictment is that they deprived him of the possibility of disclosing the nature of his paraphilic fantasies during childhood and adolescence. He was obliged to live with them in solitude until age twenty-two. Only then could he dare to reach out for help. The experience of talking, writing, and approving his own story for publication seems to have proved beneficial in bringing about a change in both the imagery and practice of autoeroticism. In addition, the use of the hormone Depo-Provera helped to alleviate his obsession.

The Value and Importance of This Sexual Biography

The narrative that follows documents Nelson's obsessions and fascinations. More than that, it explodes with the feelings and frustrations of the sexuality of paraphilia. Here is a youth aware of his difference but unable to get help and to understand what was happening to him. Despite the rage and desperation that are evident in these pages, they reveal a high order of innate intelligence and creativity which miraculously survived the fiasco of many years of misdiagnosis and miseducation. It was only after the diagnosis had been correctly made, and after effective treatment had begun, that Nelson's learning and literary abilities were released to manifest themselves in full. It was only then, and for the first time in his entire academic career, that his grades became as high as B and A. Relieved of fantasies, his mind could concentrate. For the first time it created poetry and literary prose. When Nelson writes, it is as if he is transcribing that which has already been brought into existence. The trance state of self-asphyxiation and erotic murder fantasy has become transformed into a trance state of artistic fantasy.

Is Nelson's case unique? No. There is enough anecdotal knowledge about paraphilia to indicate otherwise. The author of *Peter Pan,* for example, was a pedophile, and likewise the author of *Alice in Wonderland.* One must be impressed by the way in which they surmounted the warping of their lovemaps, alone, and with writing as occupational therapy. One must be similarly impressed by Nelson's achievements, also.

In making this book, he talked with us many times by telephone and wrote to us. He has deep concern for those who, like himself, experience paraphilic problems. His recommendations for universally available treatment must be taken seriously. Here is a man who has lived with obsession for years and is winning. Here is someone who speaks with authenticity rather than with doctrine. He delineates that which could have helped him. To ignore his advice is disaster. How often do we in the course of history have the opportunity to take leadership from someone who has lived with the potentiality for destruction and thwarted it? How often, in the thwarting, do we have the opportunity to release the sexual energy of potential genius so that it may be metamorphosed into one of the community's civilized achievements? Now the responsibility rests with us, the community, to respond in good faith.

Part One

Childhood

Part One documents Nelson's childhood. The memories from this period reveal evidence from an early age of unusual brain functioning which existed probably from birth, and which might be of either genetic or some other intrauterine origin. It manifested itself as auditory images (screaming head noises) and visual images (hoards of jostling, fighting creatures on walls and ceiling) resembling hallucinations. At night they prevented sleep unless counteracted by rhythmic, side-to-side rocking movements reminiscent of the stereotyped movements of childhood autism. In sleep there were very vivid dreams, some terrifying, and some accompanied by sleep paralysis of the transient type known also as one of the symptoms of the brain disease narcolepsy.

In addition to these various signs of brain functioning that has been atypical since prenatal life, there is also evidence of the same early origins of immunological dysfunction, namely a lifelong history of asthma, a malady known to be related to the immune system. The significance of asthma for asphyxiophilia is that both are characterized by paroxysmal breathing blockage. Whereas paroxysmal asthma attacks are not erotic, the paroxysmal discharge of the orgasm is. It is the paroxysmal nature of both that allows the two to become associated. Though no statistics are yet available, it is apparent from the reports of parents who have lost a son to autoerotic self-asphyxiation that many of them had a history of asthma.

In Nelson's early childhood, the experience of breathlessness became associated at night with bondage, for he was tied down to his crib, to prevent wandering. Bondage and breathlessness became genitally associated when, with a "pee hard," he would not be heard calling to be untied, and so would have to wet the bed. As is typical for young children, he reversed his own role as victim by, in play, trying to tie up the cat and the dog. This play became, in later years, the prototype for a more sophisticated version of bondage play with his same-aged nieces. This bondage play can be classified as a form of juvenile sexual rehearsal play—a premonition of things to come. It took the place of the more typical form of juvenile sexual rehearsal play, namely boy/girl copulatory positioning—which is widespread in the primate kingdom. Copulatory rehearsal play may be considered as an essential precursor of postpubertal heterosexual falling in love and pairbonding.

Of far greater importance than juvenile bondage play as a premonition of things to come was the catastrophe of a girl's death by drowning, another form of choking to death. The intensity of Nelson's loss was magnified by the guilt of having himself survived without having had time to disclose his true feelings, and to make amends for having treated her badly. He had dreams of himself swimming frantically under water, trying to rescue her. He was eleven years old.

1

Proclamation

This is the story of my life as an asphyxiophiliac; as such, it is the first ever written. I have used both prose and poetry to convey the love, lust, rage, self-hatred, guilt, and misery that is the peculiar madness of asphyxiophilia. I hope this candid expression of my experiences and emotions will help other paraphiles struggling with their own sexuality. This book is primarily intended for them. But it should also be read by all professionals who work with people in depth: not only sexologists but psychiatrists, physicians, educators, counselors, and politicians.

This book is for those who believe that sexual problems can be solved medically and scientifically, with compassion and understanding. Parents who want such problems to be prevented should read this book. Politicians who realize the importance of finding a cure for sex disorders and are willing to fund the necessary studies will find this book of interest, as will scientists working to make a control medicine available for sexually ill people.

Paraphiles can not help themselves unless they get help from those who will work for it. Epilepsy has a medication. So does diabetes. People with those disorders are not refused treatment and medication. They are not disbelieved and punished. All paraphiles who read this must come out to the hospitals and clinics and demand Depo-Provera, a medication which helped me in my struggle with asphyxiophilia.

I believe we need clinics for childhood paraphilias which aim to prevent them in the first place. We need hotlines for paraphiles and research programs to study the brain to find out why it malfunctions. There are many like myself waiting for help. An advanced society like ours should be able to provide that help.

For a long time I was very confused about myself. I really did not know who or what I was. I wasn't like normal members of the human race; there was something missing or malfunctioning in me. Perhaps the seeds of what I was to become in my adult life were developing all through my childhood. I know I did unusual things when I was a child, things I could not understand in myself: for instance, I tied up the cat and the dog, and then tried to strangle the cat, but the cat won and I got scratched hands. I was also bitten by the dog when I tried to tie it up. I was even tying myself up, not strangling yet, just tying myself up. All I knew was that I was crazy. I would not understand who I was until I was twenty-two.

I am an asphyxiophiliac. I started to strangle myself when I was sixteen. I didn't hang myself, however; I choked! I strangled myself in front of an angled mirror, using a nylon pantyhose. I wore a tight pair of men's 100-percent-nylon, see-through bikini underwear and pretended the whole time that a homosexual killer was throttling me. I struggled like mad in front of a mirror which was aimed at my buttocks and legs. After I choked to the point where my dizziness got too much for me, I broke off the pantyhose, fell to the floor as if I were dead, and immediately masturbated until I climaxed in a super, great orgasm. Then, and only then, was I relieved and the curse or spell was lifted for the time being. I always promised to myself that I would never do it again. But when it struck, there was no stopping it.

I could tell when I was losing control: I felt butterflies in my stomach; I smelled something burning far away; there was a pressure on my temples; and a feeling of sexual excitement began to build. These feelings got stronger and stronger until my hands began to shake, I broke out in a cold sweat, and my head was spinning. Finally, I'd lose control and would dress up and plan my own death. The excitement that I felt in my brain was similar to the feeling of speeding downhill on a roller coaster.

This addiction was impossible to fight. I fought it for seven years. At times I thought I'd won. But somehow I lost the battle every time. I was not rational when doing this sexual act. I could think of nothing but the struggle and the strangling. Of course, I knew it was not normal from the very beginning. I would be the first to admit that it was both abnormal and dangerous. I gave signals to my high school counselors, even telling one that I masturbated as much as twelve times a day. She just said that it was okay to unwind.

By the time I was twenty, I was in counseling therapy. But there was no therapy for my condition. I told the counselor with great fear that I was having terrible fantasies of stranglings and drownings when I masturbated. He just sat back and calmly said that as long as they remained fantasies, they were normal. I thought to myself, "That's rotten advice," but I was afraid to tell him this because I knew I needed help and I didn't know where else to get it. Well, I didn't believe my fantasies were normal, but I couldn't stop. When I told him that I was strangling myself for a sexual thrill of some kind, he didn't believe me. He thought I was doing it for attention.

At twenty-one, the next stage, I was getting worse and worse. I got the same attacks every month and they would last for several days in a row before I could not do it any more—until the next month. My neck had so many burns it looked like I had a ring around it. I tried throwing all of my ritual materials away—the bikinis and the pantyhose. But when I got another attack, I would find myself roaming the underwear sections of department stores to buy new pantyhose and bikinis. Then I would do it again in front of the mirror.

I called hotlines for mental health but was accused of abusing the lines by teasing and harassing the nurses with weird, bizarre stories about what I was doing. Still, I could not get away from it.

After that, I was sent to a hospital psych-ward that had a super ego and reputation. I told three so-called professionals, and their reactions were very interesting. For each head psychiatrist there were five observers listening to the conversations—medical and mental health students working on their degrees.

The first group thought that my parents sexually abused me. Wrong!

The second group thought that I might be having some kind of love affair with the building where the counselor who had sent me to the hospital worked. He was planning to kick me out of therapy because of my crazy phone calls and stories about my problem, which he didn't believe. So the group theorized that to avoid getting kicked out of the only place where I could at least talk about my problems, even if it was only to a plaster wall, I invented the whole thing and made lying phone calls so I would not be removed from the building I had become so attached to! Wrong!!

The last group simply thought that I liked to shock people. Wrong! Wrong!! Wrong!!!

And that was that. I was no better off than I was before. I knew that my curse would come back to turn me on and that my brain would go out of control again and again. Finally, I felt there was nothing left to do except to commit suicide. Everyone wanted to know *about* me, but no one wanted to know *me*. I was tired of people always wanting to hear my story but never really listening to what I said.

It was at that low point of my life that I got in contact with Dr. Money, by sheer chance. He has urged me to tell my story, not only for my own good but for that of all other paraphiles who desperately want to be understood. I want to start at the beginning, the very beginning.

2

Poems of Definition

Love to Me is . . .

Love is pain in the heart
Butterflies in the stomach
Obsession with the specific madonna
To look at her
To think of her and be unable to stop
To want to be with her while knowing it won't happen

To me love is wrong
There is usually a high price
The madonna will use you
Steal from you
Not care for you
Put on an act
And eventually go with someone else

Love to me is to be punished for love
To be laughed at for love
Love is a curse
Love should never be
Love is silly
Love is a joke

The specific madonna will not take my love
The madonna will not love me but hate me
The madonna only loves the superman
The big muscles that I don't have
The madonna will lie to you
The madonna will humiliate you

The madonna is incapable of love
All females are incapable of love
They do not like sex
They do not want love
They use you hate you and hurt you

I will never have love
I always fail
I fail because I love
I fail because I want to make love with sex
I fail because I buy her things
I fail because I am not the superman that other men are
I'm a failure at sports
I'm a failure at tests of the brain

I'm a failure because I cry
I'm a failure because I am a weakling
I'm a failure because I love and that is wrong
I'm a failure because I'm an Asphyxiophiliac

Curse

It runs your life
It controls
and masters you

You must do what it commands

You think of it always
And it thinks of you
You are obsessed with it
And it with you
It preys on you
And you must obey

The curse crushes you from within

You may think it has gone
You may think it is over
But then it comes back without warning
For it is never ending

It will haunt you until you are dead
You cannot fight it; it only gets stronger
You cannot tell anyone; they won't believe you
When you speak of its strength and its power

No one will see it, for it is invisible

It lives in your brain running it senseless
Running it, running it to pure exhaustion
It weighs on your shoulders like a ten-ton stone
Like a hungry jackal gnawing at the bone
Only when you give in is the burden eased
The hunger ceases but soon increases
It must be fed

Until you're dead

Sometimes it fools you with a long reprieve
You praise yourself and think you have conquered it
Soon it returns and is hungry again
To rule you and command you and run you
To exhaustion
Your brain overflows with endorphins
The curse of the asphyxiophiliac wrecks your life

This endless and bottomless curse can kill you
You will be breathless, lifeless, and dead
Leaving only a message of terror and confusion
To those who never knew of the curse of the asphyxiophiliac

And the curse always wins

For people can't talk about it; it is too hard
They talk about the victim after it is too late
As long as no one talks
The curse of the asphyxiophiliac
Will continue to run you until you are dead

3

My Story Starts

Seeing Things on the Walls

There once was a man who could see things on the walls
Thousands of people crowded all over the walls
They screamed and moved violently
Usually from left to right
Ear noises rang in his head
The more violent the crowds
The more noisy the ringing
Until his temples felt like they were going to implode
The ringing in the ears was loud and all around him
The things on the walls never leave him
They are with him day and night since he was very little
They get worse if he tries to fight them
They go wherever he goes
He goes wherever they go
Into the day and into the night

From the Crib

I was the last child. My mother had six children and was married three times. She had four children by her first husband: Jeff, John, Janet, and Kathleen. My brother Jeff, her first child, is twenty-five years older than I. She then got divorced and a short time afterward married her second husband, my father. A few years later, she had her fifth child, Laura. Fifteen years after Laura was born, she had me when my father was sixty-five. He died when I was two of a massive heart attack.

My mother ran the Well's School of Dance in our basement. My sisters Kathleen and Laura taught the dance classes. By the time I was born,

Kathleen was married and had left home. But Laura and a friend continued to teach the classes. I was dancing at recitals as early as three years old.

At the age of four I suffered terrible earaches that caused nerve damage to my ears and a partial hearing loss. The loss was severe enough that I could carry on a conversation only with someone standing really close by. If they were any farther than four feet away, I seemed to hear things in reverse, and sounds just weren't clear. Members of my family would get madder and madder by the minute because I needed to have things repeated all the time.

At this age, I was also plagued by hearing head noises and seeing things on the walls when I tried to get to sleep at night. The head noises consisted of a steady ringing in my brain that would not stop. The things on the walls looked like thousands and thousands of screaming, fighting people jammed into one another and covering the walls and the floors of my bedroom. It seemed that I was hundreds of feet above them, so they appeared small and numbered in the thousands. (They are with me to this very day, thousands of them all over the place.) To escape these frightening sounds and images I would rock from side to side in bed clenching both of my fists. If I remained still in bed, the head noises would scream and ring louder, and the things on the walls would be all over me.

As a result, my family couldn't keep me in the crib at night. Because I didn't want to be alone, I would sneak to the top of the stairs and sit there where I could at least be closer to the rest of the family sitting down-stairs in the front room. When I got caught, they would tie me into the crib to keep me there. One time when I refused to go to bed, my brother chased me all around the house. I was laughing, thinking that my brother thought it was funny too. But he wasn't laughing, and I got a hard spank-ing that I never forgot. Then it was up to the crib again to be tied in.

My mother would wait until I said my prayers, kiss me goodnight, and then tie me up for the night. If I needed to go to the bathroom or to get a drink, I had to yell out. One time I had to go to the bathroom so bad, but no one came when I yelled, and I finally wet the bed. Other times someone would come, but only after I called out many, many times. In the morning they would untie me so I could get up to go to nursery school.

Sometimes I would manage to escape at night from the rope that tied me in, but then someone would come up with a better way to make the knot. One time the knot was so tight that my sister had to get something sharp to cut it in the morning. I had many nightmares these nights.

Eventually I got my own bed, and it was no longer necessary to tie me in any more because my mother slept in the same room with me. We had twin beds—she slept in one and I in the other. I would often go over to her bed in the middle of the night and crawl in with her. When she fell asleep, then I could sleep too. But the next time I woke up I would find that she had gone over to the other bed just to get away from me. I would go over and crawl in with her again, but then she would move back to the other bed. This bed hopping went on and on and, no matter how hard I tried, I could not sleep with my mother. I felt all alone. I did not know how to explain this to her, so I didn't try.

A big change happened with the marriage of my mother to my stepfather. We moved to his house, and I not only had my own bed, but my own room as well. From then until about the age of nine, I would wet the bed because, for some strange reason, I had a recurring dream that I was paralyzed and could not move. Since I could not wake up to go to the bathroom, I wet the bed for many nights.

Dreams

In one of my most frequent dreams, I would be lying in the crib, trapped and tied up. I heard this steady thumping, like a heartbeat. It sounded like it was coming from downstairs in the basement and it shook the whole house. I listened as it got louder and closer to me and then I knew what it was—the furnace in the basement. Our house had a huge octopus-shaped furnace. It was round and fat like a big, bulky can that stood on the floor of the basement and reached all the way to the ceiling. It had arm-like pipes that went in all directions, plugging into the walls and ceiling to pump heat throughout the house. The inside of this monstrous thing was in flames, and the flames looked like they were sitting on top of a big block of round cheese. You could see inside just by opening a small door. In the dream, this thing would somehow come upstairs to get me, but it never quite caught me.

I had another dream once in which alligators were chasing me from the downstairs to the upstairs; it was all in slow motion. The air seemed heavier than normal, so I had to fight the slow motion effect as well as the alligators, which needed no water to swim in; they just pulled themselves along the floor of the house. I finally got upstairs and escaped.

In another dream my mother's head became detached from the rest of her body. Her body then disappeared leaving just her head sitting on a couch in the front room. She was alive, in no pain, and, in fact, was watching television. I had to feed her, but because I was so little, the only way I could get to the stove was by standing on a foot stool. I made bacon and eggs for her, but there was no way for me to get to her from the kitchen because it was blocked by a gate. She was in the front part of the house and I was in the back part of the house. So the only way for me to feed her was to shape the food into pellets and load them into a gun. The gun was attached to a tripod and was aimed at my mother. When I pulled the trigger, the pellets shot out. My mother opened her mouth, caught the food, and ate it that way. I could hear the food crunch in her mouth. This is how I fed her.

Another dream featured my real father (who died when I was two and whom I never knew or can't remember), my sister, and myself in the front yard. I was five and my sister was fifteen years older as in real life, but my father was a baby, and there we were playing with these balloons. My father was sitting on a swing that had a balloon attached to it. It slipped from my sister's hands and the balloon went up into the sky carrying my baby father away. We were unable to bring him down. I thought the dream was real, so I asked my sister how this could happen. But she didn't understand what I was talking about.

I had another dream in which all the television sets came to life. They started a revolution and took over the house. I called them TV toids. In the dream my nephew, who was two years younger than I, and my niece Janice, who was my age (four or five), were in the basement where the dance studio was. A friendly TV toid, whose name was Troy, was with us too, as well as an old TV toid that ate people. When the toids attacked, they shorted out Troy, so he was unable to fight them, and they chased us up the stairs to eat us. The octopus furnace, from earlier dreams, had ordered the toids to attack; even the washing machine and dryer came to life. We ran through the house, and it seemed like the longest house there ever was. We ran and ran until we came to a slanted track with a cart on it for us to sit in. My niece Janice and I sat in it and my nephew pushed us up the track. Why it happened that way I don't know, but this track replaced the stairs that went up to the second floor, and on the roof there was a space ship in which we were going to escape. We went up to the launch pad where the floor was straight and the cart leveled off. To the right of me I saw my two brothers adding on to the house. The dream ended before the toids ever caught up with us.

"Dressing Up"

My sister Laura got married when I was five years old. I was the ring bearer and my niece Jenny was the flower girl. After the wedding was over and Jenny had left, I saw the flower-girl dress she had worn in the living room. It was beautiful, like a miniature bride's dress. A feeling came over me. Somehow, I had to do it. I put the dress on right over my clothes and pretended that I was a girl. I thought it would be neat to be a girl, and wearing the dress gave me a feeling of happiness.

Just then, my mother came into the room. I told her that I wished I could be put into a machine that tranformed me into a girl. My mother started to crack up, and she ran into the other room to tell my brother. Everyone laughed and I felt humiliated. I jumped out of the dress right away so no one else could see.

I had a similar experience in the basement where there were many girl's dance costumes hanging on a rack. They sparkled so, I had to put one on over my clothes. It felt neat and, again, that feeling of happiness was back. It was like being a girl. I started to walk around in it and was looking at myself in the mirror when my sister Laura caught me. She didn't say anything. She just calmly took the dress off and put it away, and I never heard anything about it after that. I wanted to do it again, but I didn't dare. I was fascinated by these dresses. And I didn't know why!

My sister stayed married to her husband for only about a year. It was enough time for him to father a child, my nephew, whom he was very mean to. In fact, he was mean to everybody. He resented me and demonstrated it by pulling me up in the air by my hair. One time he came out of the bathroom and showed me his seven inch penis. He sort of jumped up and down to make the penis bounce. It was the longest damn thing on anyone that I had ever seen.

Laura and her husband with the big cock were determined to prove to themselves and to my mother that I could be forced to eat even if I didn't want to. Since the day I was born I was a picky and fussy eater. I never could stand eating with anybody. It was much safer and more comfortable for me to eat by myself and to be left alone. So to change this, their plan was to force-feed me when my mother was not around. One of them would put an arm around me and hold me in position, and the other would force-feed me with a spoon. Even though I choked and screamed, they kept shoving food down my throat to the point where I threw up. (After my sister was divorced, she used to do this same thing to her own children years later.) To escape this torture, I eventually learned to throw food I didn't like in the trash when nobody was looking.

After my sister divorced her husband, he still had visiting rights for his son, which was a joke because he did not love him. My mom and sister figured that, because of his misfortune and his crappy father, he could do anything he pleased. His father and the divorce became an excuse for his conduct. He was favored by my mom whenever he was around me, but I was just in the way at his house. Oh, at first things were all right, but he soon realized that I made a perfect scapegoat. As a result, I'd often get into trouble when my nephew did anything wrong.

Before she remarried, my sister had about three other boyfriends. Two of them resented me: I was just in the way. One time I caught one of them in bed with her. While they were both sleeping, I dressed up in an old girl's dance costume. I liked the idea of being a girl and sometimes I actually wished I was female. Of course I was caught and everyone had a nice big laugh. The whole family laughed. I hated her boyfriends, one of them in particular. When she had to baby-sit me while my mom and dad were at work, he just didn't like it when I was around. He usually swore and yelled at me. However, my little nephew could do anything he wanted and it was supposed to be cute.

The only child I had to play with was a girl who lived next door, named Edna. She must have been five or six, slightly older than I. She would tell me stories of how her adoptive parents never fed her, and I believed everything she said. My mother hated her because she would make me lose interest in playing with my cars. All I wanted to do was play with her.

Also, Edna showed me things that weren't right. She used to spit, just like her brother, on the floor, outside, or anywhere. One time I saw her go to the bathroom outside; so then I had to do it too. I squatted right there in her back yard, as if there was an invisible toilet there. In mid bowel movement my mother came out of the house and took me in. There were times when I could not go to the bathroom because it felt like there were thorns on the turds, and it hurt too much to push. I thought that I was going to have the turds in my rear for the rest of my life.

Nursery School and Kindergarden

In nursery school, I remember especially when I had to go to the bathroom. There weren't any doors to the bathroom or on the separate toilet booths. The girls would see me wipe my butt and laugh at me. Every time I went to the bathroom two or three girls would peek and watch me, and there was nothing I could do about it. One time I had a messy bowel movement and had to wipe myself several times. Two girls stood in the doorway laughing at me and would not go away. I wished they would but they didn't. So I had to wipe the mess off me, pull up my pants, and then flush the toilet in front of them.

I also remember the spankings by the teachers. They would pull down our pants and spank us with their bare hands. When the little girls were spanked, I could see their colored underwear. I couldn't help but look at them for what seemed a long time. Even though I was only five years old, I used to think of the girls' panties in my fantasies. I would make mental pictures in my mind about their yellow and pink underwear, and wish I could have such colorful underwear to wear. I just loved the panties.

At that time, the only thing I could watch and cared to watch on television was a show called "Lost in Space." I used to get all excited when the show came on and would sit in front of the television singing to myself in a whispering voice "Lost in Space . . . Lost in Space. . . ." Wow! That was my reaction when Angela Cartwright came on. She had dark brown hair and brown eyes and she wore a green dress with pink on the shoulders and sleeves and a diamond shape decorating her chest. She also wore green tights and green booties.

I would dream about Angela Cartwright's green tights and panties and the yellow tights and panties of another girl on the show, Marta Kristen. I used to dream and think about them over and over again. I watched the show all the time waiting for Angela Cartwright, as Penny, to come on. She was my favorite. So were her legs and panties. Even though I could never see the panties I would always imagine them in my head. She would scream every now and then on the show. I loved that. I was even more fascinated when both Angela and Marta would scream together.

One time I went to the movies with my sister and nephew to see a western. In the film, a man on a train is shown trying to escape his pursuers by climbing a ladder to get to the roof of the train. One of the pursuers grabs his pants and pulls them off. The man, still in his underwear, is then tied to a chair and gagged. I remember being fascinated and obsessed for weeks with his long red-striped underwear. I didn't care for the man himself, but I fantasized that this would happen to me.

When little girls at school would dress up, I would hope that the wind would blow their dresses up so I could see their underwear. Girls were always self-conscious about such mishaps. When her dress would accidentally come up and expose her pink, white, or yellow panties, a girl would grab her dress on the bottom end and hold it down while other kids yelled, "I see your underwear!" I didn't say anything or make fun, but still I watched to see her butt all covered in some spectacular yellow or white, maybe with pink flowers all over.

My dreams were full of color. I would dream that Angela and Marta, from "Lost in Space," were in my bedroom sitting on the floor. I was sitting in front of them talking and playing a game like checkers with them. It was beautiful. It was as if I knew Angela and Marta for real and they were my friends. But there was no sex, because I didn't know what it was at the time. (In fact, I didn't know what sex was until I was sixteen. Oh, I knew who was the boy and the girl, but I didn't know about how babies are made.) In the dream my bedroom was like a bedroom in a spaceship going to Mars. There were beads hanging everywhere and lots of colors were painted all over the walls.

This obsession I had for Angela's underwear made me actually believe I saw them once on a show when there was an explosion. She jumped up and I thought her underwear showed because her dress flew up. But that never happened, I learned, when I saw the show many years later. Somehow my mind seemed to see it anyways.

I couldn't help myself. That's all I wanted to think about, and I could never ask questions or talk about it, because then I was told I was being silly. I would get laughed at by my whole family. It was a joke to them but important to me.

When I was in "kitty-garden" (That's how I heard the word kindergarten), I found myself in "time out" a lot. I remember always wanting to play with the girls instead of the boys. But the girls didn't like me because it didn't look right for them to be playing with a boy who had buck teeth and who would not play with the other boys.

I liked girls, and not because I was after their underwear. But I still looked at girls. I thought they were pretty. I was never mean to them, but no one liked the idea of me talking to girls.

I was never sure why I was in time out. I knew I was crying a lot. All I ever did was cry, because no one would help me get my snow boots on and I missed more recesses than anybody. The problem was I didn't know how to tie my shoes, and I couldn't tell the right shoe from the left one; so snow boots were impossible. Another frustrating thing was that right in the middle of kindergarten class my teacher would take me to an isolated room with a table and give me puzzles to do. I couldn't stand it. I hated the damn puzzles. I don't do puzzles even now, mainly because I have never been able to put puzzles together the way they're supposed to go.

All of this was so upsetting that I got sick and developed an ulcer while still in kindergarden. As a result, I had to eat baby food, take antacid pills, and all my food had to be chopped up to help my digestion. I also had to go to the big city to see a specialist.

Anyone who had to baby-sit me in an emergency, I swear, hated doing it, but they did so for my mother or for the money. I seemed to be a problem for anyone who came into contact with me. Baby-sitters, brothers and sisters, nieces and nephews, parents—I was trouble for them all.

While I was in kindergarten I had what seemed like a million hearing tests. But I enjoyed them because the doctors would put earphones on my ears and then I had to signal them when I heard a beeping sound. I never knew what the hell all that was about either. No one ever told me anything. I spent more time taking hearing tests and going to doctors to get examined than any one else in my class.

After kindergarten, I was taken out of the public school system. I was still having trouble with my shoes. I don't know how many times I was yelled at by people who were trying to teach me how to tie my shoes. After a lot of fuss, I finally managed to tie them the right way. It must have been desperation on my part that made me get it right.

4

Poems of Time and Recollection

The Steeple Stands

When I was 2, 3, 4
I was in a family much older than I
I was born into it
I was born to a family that lives in a strange Catholic order
The church is big and red and titanic
Its steeple can be seen all through downtown
Its shadow is invisible
It scrapes the sky
When I look up at the sky
The steeple seems to move
Faster and quicker
Like never before
The clouds they drift by
With an airy mood of doom
It is like a trance
To stand
And look up at it
It feels as if the whole world is moving
And it is the clouds which are still
The steeple moves
But you don't get dizzy
You stand entranced
Until your eyes burn from the air

The steeple is in everyone's life
It looms there and sits there
Like God
The bats, the bats

There are thousands of them flying
Flying at sunset
All around the steeple
Wondering if they will attack
Attack the so-called humans
But they never do
Instead they play tag with each other
All around the steeple

It's the tallest steeple
The tallest in the city
You can see it rise above everything around
It commands, it controls
But only in the beholding
When I was 2, 3, 4, and older
Obsession with it
To stare at it
To want to control it
To be bigger than it
The world is my steeple
Which can be raised to any size and length
To open the door to a thousand dimensions
For it is a prison and I am unable to escape

Time Shaft

A tunnel flows from one end of the world to another
Time shaft it is called
It runs endlessly to another
Another world
Another universe
Another dimension
It can conquer and rule

Fast
Swift
Indestructible
The time shaft
The means to go beyond
Beyond the normal
Beyond the known

Beyond the familiar
Beyond the accepted

It leads to the unexpected
It goes beyond normal

To travel in the shaft there must be a vehicle
When you travel in the time shaft
You feel as if nothing can hurt you
You are indestructible
The tunnel spins by you
The tunnel changes color
It turns yellow to red
Red to orange
Orange to pink
Pink to green
There are mixtures of color never known before

The time shaft is a secret
Only few know of its existence

5

I Go to School

First Grade Was No Good

First grade (now at a Catholic school complete with a church) started out the same way: girls, girls, girls, and more girls. I don't know why, but I was always looking at a girl, wishing she was my sister or somebody I could play with. I was interested almost exclusively in girls. Occasionally, I made friends with a boy, but it seemed that he always moved away or had to leave school for some reason. I could talk to some boys, but only in school. Outside of school, I never seemed to fit in with them. They wouldn't let me play ball or join them in anything.

I was hardly ever invited to a birthday party, as all the other boys were. I went to one in kindergarten and maybe another in first grade, but I'm not sure of that. My own birthday party in grade two was the last party I attended for the rest of my school life. All of the boys were invited and most of them came.

In first grade I could never do anything right. Everyone else got good grades but mine always fell. My mom would be called to a teacher-parent conference at school while I was at home. When she got home, we would get into a fight, because I was accused of being lazy, watching too much television, or looking for attention. Then I would start crying all over again. It would never end. Every year from then on this would happen. My grades were a disaster. So I just gave up trying to do my work because I just couldn't get it right anyway. "He's lazy or something," they'd say.

Asking for help was impossible because then they'd say, "Oh, he's just lazy and wants us to do it for him." So I rarely got help from anyone except the occasional willing student sitting next to me. Much later, in my junior-high years, there were teachers who tried to help me, but by that time I was so far behind that it was frustrating for them to try to explain things. No one helped me when I really needed it; they all said I was the problem. My writing, for example, wasn't very good; it remained at a first-grade level through grade seven, eight, and nine.

Nothing seemed to work. So the more I couldn't succeed, the more I watched television. I could fade away into a fantasy television land. I hated to go to school so much that in the mornings I would hope that I'd get sick, that the school would blow up, or that a flood or a blizzard would hit. But these things never happened.

An aunt on my deceased father's side sometimes baby-sat me. She hated me and I hated her in turn. She wouldn't even feed me, so my mother had to give me a can of soup to take with me. She always acted like I was a pain in the neck. At least I got to go outside and run around.

This aunt died the summer before I went into second grade. At the visitation I was more interested in seeing what a coffin looked like than in anything else. Weeks later I asked my mother why we didn't see my aunt anymore, and my mother told me that she had died. Of course I knew this but I liked to hear my mother tell me that she was dead, I hated her so. In any case, my mother didn't like my deceased father's family because they treated us as if we didn't exist. They only tolerated us because of her marriage to my dad.

Second Grade: Tap-Dance Torture

Second grade was a little better in school because I was put in the front of the classroom and the teacher made sure I understood everything. That year tubes were put in my ears, and then my earaches finally stopped. Nonetheless, there were no after-school activities that I could fit into, so I'd come home to my television shows. I became an expert on "Star Trek" and "Dark Shadows" because I watched them every day when I got home after school.

The only extracurricular activity I participated in was tap-dancing lessons, which my sister taught at the dance school my mother ran. Although I hated these lessons, I took them for five years in a row, and I was in the dance recitals as well. I was never more alone and miserable than when I had to dance with the girls. I didn't really know any of them, even though I wanted to. I couldn't even get them to talk to me. It seemed they didn't like boys at that age. I felt cut off and I hated it. I was the only boy in the whole dance school.

The girls were beautiful in their pretty dance costumes with their smooth, bare legs. I, on the other hand, was dressed only in vest, pants, and tap shoes. We would all stand there side by side on the stage. I would have to watch the girls next to me because I kept forgetting my routine.

After the recital I was always told that I should have paid attention to what I was doing instead of looking at the girls while they were dancing. I would screw up the dance routines all the time. In fact it was impossible to teach me how to dance because I could never get it right.

Since I was much younger than my brothers and sisters, I got the reputation of being spoiled to death. People thought I was pushy and would treat me as if I was going to do something to them or try to take over, so they stayed away from me as much as possible. Their children would never play with me. That's the way it was at school and at dance class. Finally, the dance school closed and I didn't have any more tap-dance torture lessons.

Third-Grade Troublemakers

In third grade, things went from bad to worse. I wasn't seated in the front of the classroom anymore and I couldn't get any help from the teacher. Everyone said, "He just wants us to do it for him," which was not true. To make matters worse, I got involved with two boys who were always getting in trouble. They acted as if they liked me, and they wanted to be liked. I don't know what their problems were, but they were in the principal's office constantly.

One time, one of these boys and I sneaked through a passageway which led underneath the stairway and into a room that nobody knew about except the janitor and maybe a couple of teachers. The room was covered with dust and cobwebs. There was an old filing cabinet there and a pile of boxes full of old lost-and-found stuff which was never claimed by anybody. So we stole whatever we found in the boxes—hats, yoyos, frisbees, jackets, and other little things that you could get out of a bubble gum machine. Other kids found out what we were doing and they started going in the old storage room, too. We thought we were teaching the school a lesson, but later the school put up steel bars so no one could get in.

My parents put an end to my friendship with the two troublemakers. It was my stepfather who engineered that. He also made sure I couldn't have any friends from the neighborhood, either.

That same year I fell in love with the girl next door. Her name was Peggy and she had brown hair and brown eyes. I started loving her when I saw her go to the bathroom in the raspberry bushes behind the garage. My friend Edna somehow got into a fight with Peggy's two older sisters, Pammy and Jerri. She didn't like them and so she made fun of them. She told me all kinds of dirty things about them and wanted to spy on them. Their mother was ill and in the hospital, and their father had been killed in the Vietnam War. Therefore, they had no parental guidance. The oldest sister was the family guardian. I hadn't gotten to know them yet because my sister Laura didn't want me to play with them. Laura was always yelling at me for one thing or another.

6

The Birth of Madness

Love and War

It all began with Edna who wanted to start a war with them. So there I was in their back yard tipping over their trash cans and dumping the garbage onto their grass. The youngest sister, Peggy, saw what I was doing from an upstairs window, and she went to tell Jerri. Jerri came out and chased me to Edna's house. I tried to lock the door but was unable to because Jerri took hold of the door knob and turned it to one side so the door would not lock. Then she pulled the door open and made me come out with her. She was taller than I and had long brown hair. She took me to Pammy who had followed along with Peggy and was just a few feet away. She had long brown hair, too.

Peggy was standing next to Pammy. She was the most beautiful thing I ever saw. Her long brown hair was curly, kind of not taken care of, almost unkempt. Most of it was combed back into a pony tail and was tied with a white ribbon. She was my height and wore a white blouse which was not tucked in, blue jeans, and went bare footed. After Jerri caught me, Peggy stuck her tongue out at me. Then they all took me back to their place and made me pick up the garbage.

They looked for Edna but could not find her. I didn't say much, except that I was sorry and that Edna had told me to do it. They didn't yell at me. They just wanted to know who the girl was. Peggy hid behind her sisters not saying anything. She didn't know I had seen her go to the bathroom in the raspberry bushes and then wipe her cute little butt with the leaves off the trees. I felt weird about her.

On another day Edna wanted to continue the fight with them. To think that I was talked into doing her bidding again! She didn't like Peggy, so when Peggy was in my yard Edna convinced me to capture her. I seized her by putting my arms around her. We were face to face and I discovered how soft she was. I must have frightened her because she screamed and sounded like she was going to cry. It was the first time I heard her voice and I thought it was beautiful. She struggled to escape and easily slipped from my grasp. Then I grabbed her left arm and tried to pin her. But she was too strong for me. Within seconds she broke my grip and almost yanked me to the ground as she pulled away from me. She kicked Edna in the leg and then ran away from us.

I felt like I had been punched in the stomach. I was afraid that I might get into trouble for attacking her. At the same time, I was madly in love with her. A new sensation came over me. It was as if I smelled something burning, although I knew there was nothing on fire. I felt pressure on my temples and I had butterflies in my stomach. I was shaky, nervous, excited, and scared at the same time. My madness, perhaps. I thought, what have I done? Why did I do that to her? What is wrong with me?

I told Edna that I wasn't going to fight the war any more. At least, I wasn't going to fight Peggy. Edna was disgusted with me. "You like her. Don't you?" she said sarcastically. I denied it of course. "Yes, you do!" "No I don't!" I countered. I never admitted that I was in love with Peggy. I was really sorry about what I had done. I wish I knew what had gotten into me.

In the end, we all became friends and started playing together. One of the sisters tried to teach us how to smoke cigarettes and blow the smoke out of our nose and ears. I choked on the cigarettes so I gave up. Edna did it really well, but Peggy couldn't or wouldn't try it. Her two older sisters were experts at it. It turned into a joke, especially when the one tried to teach us how to do it. They smoked all the time.

I don't think Peggy liked me because she didn't have a chance to get to know me. My stupid family didn't help. I got in trouble with my sister because she caught us smoking even though she smokes herself. She had me on my hands and knees crying and begging her not to tell my mom what I did. Of course, somewhere along the line I was told not to play with such a trashy bunch of girls as the Trenery girls. But when I saw Peggy, I couldn't help but look at her.

Finally, without warning and with no farewells, the so-called trashy family moved away. Peggy, my sweetheart hopeful, was gone. I heard nothing of her until the news broke that she had drowned while swimming at the pond. That's how my fascination for the word asphyxia would come into play.

Peggy vanished while swimming with her sisters at a nearby pond. A massive search party combed the entire area including the parking lot, bath house, playground, and pond. Finally, she was found by a scuba diver at the bottom of the pond in only five feet of water. She was lying face up and had been submerged for about thirty-five minutes. The story made the front page of the newspaper and the radio and television news.

Her mother was unable to attend the funeral because she was in the hospital, near death. Mardy, the oldest sister who was responsible for Peggy, almost had a nervous breakdown. She never could escape the guilt she felt.

After Peggy's body was found, the authorities were not able to piece together exactly what had happened. It was a hot day and the beach was jammed with swimmers. Peggy and her girlfriend Lil were both making backward summersaults into the water from the end of the pier. The last time they did it Lil went first, then Peggy. When Lil came up from the water and cleared her blurred vision, she noticed that Peggy was not on the pier. With all the children crowding the beach, it was impossible to spot her. Lil thought that she must have gone to the playground again. That's what anyone would have thought. Mardy was on the beach with her two-year-old son. She had just come out of the water herself. Lil's older sister was with her and was about to take the boy to the kiddy pool.

The final theory was that Peggy flipped backward into deep water far out from the end of the pier. The fact that she was found on the bottom in a face-up position suggested that she struggled frantically to get back to the surface. She must have held her breath for as long as she could. Her legs were stuck in the sand as if she had tried to scramble up the slanted sandy hill that dropped off into the deep end of the pond. It was all dug up and the water was sandy and clouded as if some commotion had taken place on the bottom.

Maybe if I had been there, I could have saved her. But I can't swim. I would have drowned with her. If I had only seen it happen, I could have told someone. I could have told Lil; then she could have gotten the lifeguard. But it didn't happen that way. Peggy died hating me. I never said I was sorry to her. I never gave her any flowers for what I had done to her. I missed the drowning accident and the funeral. They say it was the biggest funeral in the county. I didn't find out until it was over, but I was very calm and did not cry.

I used to try to imagine her nude body drowning underwater and I wondered what it was like to drown. I started having dreams about swimming underwater and drowning. In one dream my room became a monster fish tank filled with giant goldfish. I was swimming desperately, searching everywhere for Peggy. I could breathe underwater like a fish and didn't need any kind of air tank.

Then I started to masturbate, but I'm not sure exactly when or what the first fantasy was, if there was any at all. The first orgasm I ever had was sometime after her death. But her effect on me started long before those first fantasies or that first orgasm. I loved her ever since I saw her wiping her cute little butt with the leaves off the trees.

After she drowned I could think of nothing else for a while. I was somehow drawn to it. I kept seeing the image of her swimming in the water by herself and then she would somehow just sink where I couldn't see her anymore. Her hair was long, brown, and in a pony tail that was kind of curly and messy from playing. I would imagine her swimming along and suddenly being sucked into the depths below.

In my dreams, I watched her from above, not from underwater, as if I were just a couple of feet away from her. She just sank. The "Dreamchase" dreams recurred every now and then, but there were other dreams before that—and after. These were also underwater dreams. I still had the recurring dream of being paralyzed and unable to move when I would wet the bed. But now in these paralysis dreams, I was underwater and I thought I was going to drown. But when that was about to happen, and I couldn't hold my breath any longer, I discovered that I could breathe under water. I saw other people underwater with no air tanks and they could not do what I was able to do. It was as if I had synthetic gills. I would swim and watch other people drown, mostly girls.

Peggy, I Love

Peggy was first
She had brown hair and brown eyes
Peggy was shy
She was cute
And beautiful
The Peggy I love
It was such a weird love
I never felt it before
I had butterflies in my stomach
And pressure on my temples
I smelled something burning
But there was nothing on fire
My heart was on fire
Oh it burns, oh it burns
My hands sort of shook
And all this happened when
I held her by the hand and the wrist
I felt love
At her first scream
It was a head rush of some kind
She had the most beautiful scream
I had ever heard
The Peggy I love

Then Peggy moved away
And I never saw her again
She sort of vanished from my brain
When she drowned
I didn't grieve
I felt that head rush again
And dreamed of her drowning underwater
In my mind she drowned over and over
She went deeper and deeper
Farther underwater
Until she disappeared

Oh Peggy, I'm sorry
I didn't really mean it
I didn't mean to scare you the way I did
If I could only tell you
If you only understood
Now you never will
Peggy I love you . . . .

Beyond That Door

There is the door with its four corners and sides
There is that door with its six-foot size
A rectangle so tall
Could not possibly roll like a ball
But nothing surprises me any more
For anything can happen beyond that door

I opened the door and inside was my bedroom
Though the lights were out, I still could see
But it was a vision of weirdness to be
For my room was invaded by leviathans
It was full of unbelievable beasts
Which though familiar were not the same
For they were goldfish that were ten-feet long
There was no water, they swam through the air
They swam as if lazy and bored as they were
I was thunderstruck but I did not run
For I was fascinated by this strange fun
There were three-foot bullfish

As harmless as could be
They were painless—this must be a dream
It was so real and colorful too
I was really standing there as if it were true

There were green fish, yellow fish
And orange fish too
For it was a museum of wiggling lore
As I walked into my very own room
I felt no water, yet they were swimming above my head
Then I tried to get out and I got pulled in the air
But I could not see anything holding me there
Then I just started swimming with the rest of the fish
Swimming through the air, floating in air
My excitement was crazy and my stomach was swaying
Swaying and swishing tickling me like crazy

The fish ignored me and just swam around my room
I didn't swim really, I just floated with them
Around and around and around and around
My door was still open
I could see the rest of the house
I saw my mother and step-father sitting
Sitting in the front room unaware of what was happening
I wanted to get down but I didn't know how
For I was still floating around and around

I called out to them hoping they would hear me
But they didn't hear, they just watched TV
Then I started to go faster and faster and faster
I was flying around my room at super fast speed
The fish didn't notice me
They just lazily swam right through air
As I was passing them over and over again
I tried to grab at one
But it slipped through my fingers
I tried to grab at my bed or dresser
But my arm wasn't long enough
I got dizzy and dizzy and dizzy
I woke up and my bed was all wet

7

Before the Replicas

Deaf Beauty

Shortly after Peggy died, I fell in love with a beautiful eight-year-old deaf girl with blonde hair and blue eyes. She lived in the country near my sister, who had a mobile home in a trailer court. She couldn't talk and, as far as my sister was concerned, she acted too wildly. I wanted to play with her, but my sister, with her negative attitude, made me miserable. But the deaf beauty and I were really friends, for as long as it lasted.

When I first fell in love with her, she slapped me in the face because she thought I was going to hit her, but I didn't. My sister bawled me out because the deaf girl was still my favorite person, my best friend even, and I wanted her and wanted to be around her. So I had to sneak off to play with her in a field in the back of her house. We didn't talk because we couldn't understand each other. We just chased each other around the field and a junk yard that was nearby.

Once she fell down and I looked at the scab on her soft wrist. I touched it and she let me examine it. I was hoping she wouldn't cry, and she didn't. She never cried because she tripped and fell all the time. She acted like a maniac sometimes. She always rode her bike all over the neighborhood. She would try to talk to people, but she couldn't because the only sounds she could make were those loud noises that I just loved to hear. She squealed and softly hummed and her words were like musical notes with no lyrics to them. She was beautiful!

My stepdad didn't want me to continue my friendship with her, so finally he whipped me with his belt right in front of her. She had a funny look on her face when he hit me. After that embarrassing incident, she moved away and I hardly ever saw her again. I cried all night long when I found out she was gone. I never forgot her; I loved her so much. My family told me that for a boy my age love was silly and ridiculous. I was told that I should think more about my mom and be more concerned about my school work than that dumb deaf girl.

My brother John, the second oldest, wasn't like the rest of them. He even took me to the deaf girl's new house. But I was afraid to stay and play with her because I might get into trouble. I just had had enough. She lived too far away, anyway. But then my sister, I couldn't believe it, made fun of me because I didn't stay. So I just said, "Well there was some kind of smell in the house that I didn't like, so I wouldn't let him leave without me." And that lie seemed to satisfy everyone. I always remembered, however, the time when the deaf beauty and I sat on the old mattress that was in the junkyard in the field in the back of her house. She always wore orange. Every day she wore orange.

Kids at School

At school, I was still thought of as lazy because I just couldn't keep up with the rest of the class. On the playground I was everybody's favorite target. These kids never missed an opportunity. For example, three boys rubbed my face in the snow bank and, another time, threatened to dunk my head in the toilet bowl. I was always the one who got his lunch stolen and then had nothing to eat. I got my hat stolen off the top of my head three times, and I was slapped on the school bus.

These pranks were always engineered by the same kid. I complained constantly to the teachers, but nothing was ever done about it. The teachers would just say that I was looking for attention. I even got into a wrestling match with two other boys and ended up breaking my shoulder. It sure did hurt. When tests were given to me, I promptly flunked them because I did not know what was happening any more.

In the fourth grade the kid who was after me decided to give me a break and pick on other kids. One time he brought a dead rattlesnake to school and chased girls with it, and of course the teachers did something about that. He found a dead bat and started flashing that around. Then he got into real trouble because panic-stricken parents were afraid that children who had touched the bat might get rabies. No one got sick, but they still took the bat and analyzed it to prove it harmless. He did not make fun of me any more. When he left the school for good we parted as friends, though I never could figure out why. Later he died in a car crash in which his head went right through the dashboard and into the car engine.

That year five boys from the same family came to my school but stayed for just one year. Rob was in grade six, Fred in grade five, Phil in my grade, Clem in grade three, and Mark in first grade. The school treated every one of them like shit because they were new. Everyone hated Phil, but he really wasn't a bad guy. He was picked on because of the family's financial situation as well as their social standing in the community. The parents of most of the children at this school were big shots in the church, the community, or both. The fathers, in most cases, owned a business or title of some kind. It was a really weird year with those boys. They fought back. But they didn't return the next year, and that was the last we saw of them.

Of course, I can't forget the day Nixon was reelected as President of the United States. On election day, a bunch of troublemakers and I went around asking others in our classes, "Are you voting for Nixon or McGovern?" If a boy answered "Nixon," we would make him a member of the team. But if he answered "McGovern," either he was put head first into the garbage can and left there or his head was dunked into the toilet bowl full of someone's pee.

I did not participate in the garbage-pail and toilet-bowl antics, but I watched them happen. Actually my mom and dad voted for McGovern, so I was not part of a "Nixon family." When the wild boys asked me whom I was supporting, I would say "Nixon," so I didn't get dunked or dumped in the can, and I could be a member. But I lied, partly because I knew what they would do if I said "McGovern." The other kids they asked did not know what was going on when they answered. Most of the families at this Catholic school were for Nixon anyway.

It's too bad that I had the same teacher for fourth grade as I did for third. One of my problems is that my family name starts with a letter near the beginning of the alphabet. Since the seating arrangement followed reverse alphabetical order, I was always in the back of the room. The time I did best in school was when I was right up front where I could hear clearly.

Again there were girls I knew and liked, but I did not dare let anyone know that at the time. There was just one whom I used to play with at recess, but she moved away and was not at school any more. She was really quiet, and she didn't mind hanging around with me. But of course I lost her. I can't seem to get any girl to like me long enough or, if one likes me, she seems to move away.

I got into a lot of trouble in fourth grade when a bunch of girls surrounded me and screamed and threw stuff at me. I was not turned on by it. When I tried to tell the teachers about it, they didn't do anything. While the teachers ignored us, the girls kicked me and screamed more at me.

I couldn't tell anybody about it. One girl put me into a headlock. I tried to get help, but nothing happened. So I made up a story and lied in hopes of getting somebody—anybody—into trouble, especially the girl who put me into a headlock. But that didn't work. Instead, I got put into time-out for lying. The teacher called up my mom that night and I got yelled at some more. And I thought I liked girls!

Headaches and Nosebleeds

That year I started to get very severe headaches which no one seemed to understand. They were so bad that I had to lie down for a long time. They came on very suddenly and made me sick, and took a long time to go away. I couldn't play or even keep my eyes open. It hurt on my temples and in the back of my head. It was as if I had gotten struck by a baseball bat in the back of the head. My mother put Vicks cream on my temples before I went to bed at night, so my head would be clear when I woke. She was trying to help me but it didn't work. It seemed like I had these horrible headaches everyday; they were so bad that sometimes I wished I could die. The problem persisted until the beginning of fifth grade. Then, the doctor said they were sinus headaches and he gave me some pills. The headaches did finally stop, but it took months.

No sooner did the headaches disappear than I started getting nosebleeds. I would be standing somewhere minding my own business, when I would notice a red polka-dot on my shoe; then another polka-dot would appear on the floor right next to my shoe. When I asked my mother what was happening, she brought out a cold wash cloth. I was instructed to sit in a chair, tilt my head back, and hold the wet cloth on my nose to stop the bleeding. Soon it stopped, until the next time.

One morning I woke up and felt something funny on my face. I looked in the mirror and saw a dark red road of dried blood exiting out of one nostril and running down my face to my ear. I turned and looked at my pillow and saw a blood stain where my ear was. It didn't scare me this time. It somehow fascinated me. I cleaned the crusty, dried blood off and had fun doing it.

After all of the headaches and the nosebleeds, something happened to my memory of Peggy. I totally forgot about her and blacked out the entire time with Peggy and her sisters. A complete blank. Nothing. I didn't even try to remember because I didn't know it had happened. I was unable to recall that anyone I knew had drowned. It had never happened as far as my memory was concerned. She didn't exist. My love and my obsession with her were gone.

But instead, my obsessions with the replicas would begin. I started becoming attached to girls who were replicas of Peggy, even though I didn't remember her. It would be years before I was able to figure out why I was mad about them and who they really represented. For a long time, I had no idea what was happening to me, nor any explanation for my weird behavior.

Dreamchase

I used to have a dream of a bike chase
I'm chasing a girl
Who is way ahead of me
When I get close
She gets farther away
She seems to ride her bike
Much faster than I
I can never see her face
I can only see her from behind
She has long brown hair
A little messy and curly
Somehow or another
I was in love with her
I had to have her
But I didn't know why
Every year I would have a dream chase
Not the same dream exactly
But a continuation of the last chase
In a different place
I always lost her in the end
I lost her every time
I wonder who she is
I wonder, I wonder

Sleep If

Sleep *if* only
When that *if* comes
Sleep can be lonely
But it can be heaven
If only the dreams
Wouldn't be so mean
If I could sleep
And have nice dreams

I wish to sleep
Quietly and peacefully
Without mean dreams
I wonder what sleep is like

Without any dreams?
Then I would be dead
I would be free

Death is a Gift

Death used to be a fear
To think of death was a sin I was told
For life was supposed to be precious I thought
But life for me is misery
Death no longer remains a fear
Death is welcome
Death is relief
Death is peace
Death is serenity
Life is torture
Life is meaningless
Life is the sin
The sin that justifies death

My heart is never happy
It has had many injuries
It has been repaired many times
It has been scarred and maimed
It is full of holes and cracks
It is dying, dying
It wore out even though I am young
I feel like an old man today
What will I be tomorrow
A prisoner I am
A prisoner of life
I must escape
I can't stand it any longer
For I am unable to get any stronger

I was told that suicide is the easy way out
If that is so, then that is the way to go
For who wants to suffer?
Not I, not I
I want to leave this meaninglessness
There must be peace

There must be sleep
I like to sleep
It eases the pain
Those who have escaped are the winners
They are free of the pain of today
The pain of living is like shovelling quicksand
Life, you slowly fade away with misery and pain
Death, you go quickly and safely away
Death is a gift, a treasure of escape
To peace and sleep without dreams and thoughts
To be at rest
Without cause of worry or fault

Part Two

Puberty and the Teen Years

The memory of the catastrophe involving the drowned girl became subject to a blackout on recall. The memory was not retrieved again, and explicitly recognized, until young adulthood. In the meantime, however, it manifested itself, unrecognized, in endowing the imagery of death by asphyxiation with sovereignty over the orgasm. Fantasies and dreams of asphyxiation, usually by either drowning or strangulation, engaged both the self and partners as victims: this is an antipodean duality which is a basic principle of the paraphilias. When a fantasy took hold at night, as a dream, it would wake up the sleeper and demand to be concluded by orgasm. It might demand an orgasm, insatiably, as many as four or five times a night, and more again, the next day—which is not uncommon in paraphilia.

Eventually the fantasies of self-asphyxiation were carried out as rituals. There, in front of a mirror, pulling the dance tights around his neck, Nelson would metamorphose into a girlish gay boy being stalked by a homosexual killer who would cut off his breath, and leave him dead. Of course, he would come alive, and the second or antipodean death, namely of a partner, would immediately follow, but in fantasy only. This latter fantasy was typically heterosexual. The actresses in the heterosexual fantasies appeared as if they had a life of their own. They could not be commanded to appear, nor to change roles. Some of them were fantasy representations of public figures, like movie stars, and others were local "replicas" of the drowned girl. For each of them, in turn, Nelson had an intense infatuation, but it was always love unrequited.

8

Invasion of the Fantasies

Something Is Wrong with Me

By the time puberty began I was masturbating once a day to fantasies of both boys and girls being strangled. The boys all had to have a girlish look and they always smoked first. Then two mysterious hands would come and strangle them. That's all there was to it, not any sex stuff yet. However, I did become sexually attracted to the tits and butts of my fifth-grade teacher and two teachers from the sixth grade who taught fifth-grade reading and English. In my fantasies, they were dressed in pretty clothes and were smoking cigarettes when a waterpipe or electrical cord would appear behind them and wrap around their necks. As they struggled their underpants would show. When they gasped their last breath and died, I would have an orgasm. All three teachers had brown hair, which turned me on. Brown hair was the best. They were really good looking women and all of them were in their twenties.

I went into fifth grade labeled emotionally disturbed. I was still a good three years behind in all subjects and I wrote as though I were still in first grade. But no one bothered to find out about my fantasies and how they interrupted my learning.

There were two new girls in my class that year and both of them liked me, but I didn't like them for some reason. They scared me, so I stayed away from them, but I did talk to them from time to time.

This was also the year that I got braces on all my teeth. After I got home from the orthodontist, I threw up all over the place. My mouth was sore for a long time and all my food had to be chopped up. I was the only one in the class who had braces that came complete with head-gear. I soon quit wearing that when the other kids started calling me either the "monster of metal teeth" or "tinsel teeth." Once again, I was being made fun of.

Now they had another excuse to exclude me from games. However, if I didn't get excluded from playing because of the braces, I would get kicked out because I kept missing the ball. The two girls who seemed to like me ended up moving to another school. This time I was glad that I hadn't gotten involved with them. I didn't have to miss them, because we had never become friends.

At this time I saw an episode from the "Cannon" detective series in which a beautiful girl was strangled. The whole time she was choking, the camera focused on her beautiful legs. You could hear her airless gasps, but her beautiful bare legs didn't kick or even move. This was to be a scene that I saw many times in my fantasies in which I myself would be choking cute girls.

The girl's purse and a bottle of pills dropped by her feet while she was choking to death. The tip of the dress she had on was sexy and her legs had nylons on, I think. After she was dead the killer still held her up so she was standing. The camera remained on her legs when he bent down, picked up her purse and pills, and then wrapped his arms around her pretty legs and picked her up. The first time I pictured this episode in my masturbation fantasy, I was in the role of Marta Kristen from "Lost in Space." I imagined Angela Cartwright, also from "Lost in Space," as the murdered woman in later masturbation fantasies.

Then I found myself liking to look at the pretty young legs of my fifth- and sixth-grade teachers, and I began seeing them in my fantasies. Before I knew it, I was masturbating all the time. When I sat on the toilet at home, I masturbated with this type of fantasy and I also did it before going to bed. The orgasm felt incredible; it was a new feeling that I had discovered and that feeling was great. It made me sleep better and relax better, too. Sometimes I used a boy in a fantasy, but he had to have long enough hair to make it work. Boys didn't stay with me long. I soon went back to girls.

Fifth grade also marked the year that I started having temper tantrums and fighting back. This is something my pediatrician had told me to do a long time ago. Every time I saw him, he would say, "Fight your own battles." So I did. It got me nowhere, but I soon become infamous for my maniac's temper. The tantrums included actions like throwing things, yelling and screaming, and swearing out loud. I would be sent to the office as punishment for fighting. Even when I fought, everyone cheered for the other guy. "Hit him harder!" they'd shout.

My sisters loved to see me punished. They kept telling my Mom, "Hit him harder, hit him some more, and don't let him watch television any more." The school's opinion was that I was spoiled and that's why I wouldn't do my homework. And my trouble would begin again. It never seemed to end. In all of this I had learned that there was something wrong with me. I was half-brained, retarded, or something, and no report card gave information to the contrary.

Sixth grade started out with an argument between my mother and the sixth-grade teacher. My report cards started to look a little better. I got more help but the grade never seemed to improve. It never got any higher than a C-minus but never any lower than a D-minus. Now I was allowed to play in the ball games at recess, so I thought things were improving somewhat.

It was a better year and I had more friends. Two other kids and I even wrote a play, and kids from the sixth grade were in it. At the end of the year they had a cake and punch for me because it was my idea. I'm surprised it turned out the way it did considering that my parents didn't get to see it. They had to fly down to Houston and help my sister who was sick because she had just had a baby. She had started messing up her life then and hasn't been too well ever since. I stayed next door with the neighbors who bent over backwards for me, even though they didn't have to. When my mother offered to pay them, they wouldn't take it.

The girl and her mother with whom I stayed while my parents were gone were both in my fantasies, too. I used to pretend that the girl was my baby sister while I was with them for the two-week period. I remember my ulcer drove me crazy; I had so much gas and I didn't eat much. I must have lost ten pounds.

My Brother's Religion

Meanwhile my brother John, who was good to me, was attempting the impossible, and that was to convert me into a Jehovah's Witness. He had become one himself, and this would cause great upset. I never told him that I masturbated because he said it was unclean, and he showed me passages in the Bible which condemned it. My brother is twenty-four years older than I am. However, he is the only brother in the family who has ever treated me like a brother. He and I would go to the parks and watch television together. We talked all the time about things that no one else would ever know. It was a special relationship. It didn't seem like he was so much older than I.

He had a room full of machines—like the ones in old Frankenstein movies. He was also into chemistry and astrology. He did all kinds of incredible things. He had a nonsense box with blinking orange lights that I always liked. Later on when I stayed with him in his apartment he would turn on the nonsense box and I would be hypnotized by the blinking lights. I went to sleep that way without any problem.

I was allowed to turn on the machines too, and they would emit fire and sparkling lighting. My brother would show me how to change colors with chemicals and how to make foam. He took me lots of places and he never yelled at me. We were close friends.

One time when I was only five years old, my brother and I were hiking in the woods by the water. I saw what looked to me like a playground that had been freshly black-topped and would be fun to run on. So I ran toward it and was so fast that my brother was unable to warn me. As soon as I got to the "playground," I fell right through it. I found myself in a pool of black shit and sank down until it was over my head. My brother pulled me out by grabbing my hand, and then I saw that I was standing next to a waste treatment plant. I was a mess. My brother took me to the water and washed me off. I could have suffocated, if he hadn't pulled me out as fast as he did.

Then one day, all of a sudden, my mother would not let me see him any more. When I asked her the reason for this restriction, all she said was that he was going to a different church and we didn't belong to it. I would walk to church with him when I stayed over at his place on Saturday night. Now that was no longer allowed. Well, then he hardly came around at all, not even at Christmas time. It was the same at Easter, Thanksgiving, and birthdays.

Finally my mother let me see him again and he seemed to be the same person as always. He had quit smoking, which I thought was good. One night when I was going to stay over, my mother had just dropped me off, and then—I don't know how it started—they had one of their greatest arguments. It was about whose personal religion was right. It didn't change my love for my brother, but it sure was weird. Of course no one ever cared in the least what I was thinking and feeling about the family. They seemed to think I wasn't even aware of what was going on.

Soon my brother and I began seeing each other more often to study the Bible. We read from a book of Bible stories called the "Great Teacher Book," which was about Jesus. It was a good book and I learned that the stories told by the Jehovah's Witnesses were the same as the ones told at St. Noel's Catholic School. In one month I learned more about the Bible than anyone at St. Noel's did for the whole eight years. I understood the Bible very easily. It was very clear. When I went home and told my Mom she would get angry, as though it were my fault that my brother told me these things about the Bible and Jesus. We would yell at each other. My Mom would ask "Did John tell you to come home and treat me this way and mouth off to me?" I used to have nightmares about Jesus and Moses and Bible stories. If I didn't quiet down when my Mother told me to, eventually my stepdad would put in his two cents worth and end up yelling at me. Of course I yelled back. That automatically made everything my fault because you are not supposed to treat parents that way. So that's another of my many, many sins. "Honor thy father and thy mother," the Bible says. That's all my mother would tell me among other such things to prove my unworthiness and unrighteousness.

I used to get dozens of things for Christmas, and sometimes I wished I didn't, because my mother used it as a weapon. She would say, "If you don't get good report cards, then you don't love me, do you?" or "If you loved me, then you wouldn't talk to me this way." "If you this" or "If you that." It went on and on.

My brother took me to seminars, assemblies, and meetings of Jehovah's Witnesses until I found that I didn't like it. But what the hell, I couldn't have any friends at home because my stepdad wouldn't let me. I could play with this girl, Edie, who lived next door to my brother, but she got into trouble all the time; so when I was with her, then I became her scapegoat. In any case, I had trouble getting time to play with Edie, because I was always at an assembly or something with my brother. So I didn't have much of a social life, no matter where I was.

The Birds and the Bees

My brother John gave me a book called *Your Youth! Getting the Best of it?* It was the first time I read about the birds and the bees. I was about twelve or thirteen years of age, and I still didn't understand what intercourse and premarital sex were, nor was I familiar with most other things in the book. Although I did know what masturbation was, I thought that premarital sex was just kissing and that homosexuals were boys who kissed each other. I did not connect masturbation with intercourse or even with sex or loving. Even though I masturbated often, I still didn't know the word "orgasm." All I knew was that I was committing a horrible sin.

Finally, I decided to confess this "sin" to my mom, and so I told her that I was hooked on masturbation. My mother started yelling at me and accused me of getting my crazy ideas from reading my brother's book. She said, "So you think you're hooked do you? This is the book where you are getting your crazy ideas!" I guess that took care of that. I could never talk about anything serious without getting yelled at. I suppose it would have made a lot of sense to commit suicide and that would have taught them a lesson, but then they wouldn't have learned a thing from it. Nobody ever does.

When I read the book I did learn something about homosexuals. I learned that when they play with each other they masturbate each other's sex organs. From this I derived the false notion that masterbation would turn me into a homosexual. The book was very clear on homosexuality, but the rest of it I did not understand. I had no idea what fornication or all the other stuff meant, nor did I know how a baby was made. I just didn't have the brains to connect sex with masturbation, fornication, or homosexual acts.

The book was written as though you already knew what it was all about. All I understood was that I would not go to Catholic heaven or the new paradise of the Jehovah's Witnesses. I would either be in Catholic hell or would just cease to exist.

Tyranny and Fantasy

The sixth-grade teacher I had was new to the school. She was much older than the previous sixth-grade teacher who had to leave because she was having a baby. There was no room for older women in my fantasies.

Petty kissing was beginning to get into my fantasies by the end of the sixth-grade school year. After the kissing, the boy would strangle the girl. The actors for these fantasy scenes came from a wide range including a boy and a girl who were brother and sister in school, and Melissa Gilbert and Melissa Sue Anderson from "Little House on the Prairie." "Little House" had aired for the first time and it was on every Wednesday night. In some of the fantasies, Melissa Sue and I were lovers. We would go through a time machine and strangle girls I knew in school, and then we would escape in the time machine so we couldn't get caught.

I used to strangle my three nieces in my fantasies, too. They're the daughters of my oldest sister, Janet. Each of them is blonde and blue eyed, and around the same age as I am. I didn't love them like nieces; I lusted for them and I thought they had great bodies. Every other month or so my family and my sister's family would get together. Either we would go to St. Louis, where they lived, or they would come here.

When my three nieces and I got together, sparks would fly because they were always getting punished for little things, like stealing a cookie or breaking something that belonged to my mom. They didn't do these things on purpose; they were just accidents. My stepniece and nephew on my dad's side broke stuff all the time and that was okay, but my sister really was hard on these three girls. They were often sent to their rooms when we were at their house, usually because they mouthed off to their mom. The problem was that they weren't allowed to talk above a whisper.

To make them easier to control, their parents underfed them. When I stayed at their house in St. Louis a few days, I found that I was underfed, too, and was hungry all the time. In the middle of the night the girls showed me how they would sneak around and grab food and soda pop. We would then go back to our rooms and have a quiet little party. Before we did this the girls had to make absolutely sure their parents were asleep, and this was done by Morse Code. They tapped from the room they slept in to the room I slept in. After the signal, I got my small flashlight and went over to their room. Then we had our feast. Sometimes they stole food and pop during the day and stashed it in their room before nighttime. If they had been caught the father would have killed them. I had seen him punish them before. He hit them with his fists until their skin turned red. It was unbelievable sometimes.

I was constantly masturbating while fantasizing about my nieces. It would start with the oldest, Pam, then Jenny, and finally Kim. In the fantasy I would have sex with each of them and then strangle them all in a row, from oldest to youngest. I would get an erection even if I just thought of them. Then I'd have to masturbate again. I loved them, but I lusted for them too. When we were young, and the three of them would stay at my house, we would play strangling-murder games with one another. One of the girls would use this old camera and pretend she was making a movie of me strangling another girl. Then I would carry her body and hide it on the bed. We would take turns doing this.

All the imagined stranglings ended in orgasms for me. Everybody smoked in the fantasies before any form of strangling occurred. Another fantasy featured a beautiful girl in a space suit out on a space walk. A mysterious hand came and pulled the oxygen cord off, suffocating her. Once dead, she floated away, with her eyes open forever. It was even arranged for her to be able to smoke a cigarette or a woman's cigar in the spacesuit prior to her asphyxia due to suffocation. It had to be done that way, in that form.

I used to sit and watch my genitals turn red during the fantasy and the orgasm. Then I would watch the testicles move by themselves as they tried to go back to normal. I was fascinated by how the round things would rise up, and I wondered if something was alive in there with a brain and everything.

I had two fantasies in which a priest from school was strangled. This happened when I discovered that he was a regular cigarette smoker. I saw him do it in the principal's office while talking to the principal who was a nun. In those two fantasies there was no nudity, sex, or kissing. I would not have been doing it with the priest anyway because I detested him. I thought he was wrong for being a priest and smoking. What a hypocrite! In the Bible, according to the Jehovah's Witnesses, smoking is a defilement of the flesh. I myself do not smoke but have tried. I didn't like it.

My sister and brother-in-law smoked all the time. It didn't matter if they were at their own house, or if they were visiting at ours. They smoked all the time, and it made me sick. It gave me terrible asthma attacks. I can remember having asthma attacks all my life and hardly being able to breathe. Medication doesn't help when they're really bad, and I'd have to go to the emergency room.

Rebel

I had started taking piano lessons in the third grade. By the sixth grade it was obvious I wasn't making any progress. I didn't practice, so I didn't get very far. In three years I progressed only half a year. The reason I didn't practice was that I was constantly yelled at for banging on the piano keys. It wasn't my fault. Because of my hearing problem, I heard the notes normally when I played the keys the way I wanted. When I tried playing more softly, I couldn't hear the damn notes. So what was the point? The piano teacher constantly scolded me for banging on the keys. I couldn't tell them what was really wrong because I didn't know myself. I got so sick of the yelling and being humiliated over and over again, I avoided the piano. Sometimes I would purposely forget my piano books or the lesson, or I would lie or do something else to avoid being punished for something I had no control over.

Seventh grade was a major change for two very important reasons. First, a good third of the entire class left and went to the junior high school in the public school system. They were able to say a permanent goodbye to their old Catholic school of parochial pettiness and hypocrisy. Second, we had a male teacher for the first time in the history of our class. In fact, we had two male teachers.

They were of course worthless for me because of the way I was labeled and my failure to compete with the rest of the class. I flunked tests, messed up the assignments, and was still a good three or four years behind academically.

Four new faces were in class that year; they came from other schools. Two of them were to revolutionize the behavior pattern in everybody in the seventh grade. This was not for the better but, of course, for the worse. Since they were nothing but trouble, it would be only natural that they and I should get together, and we made quite a mess of things that year. Most of the time I was their enemy.

There was also a drastic change in my attitude toward girls. Now I wanted them and I would not be put off. Predictably, the first girl had brown hair and brown eyes. I didn't know at the time why I was attracted to girls that looked like that, but I sure was. When she sat next to me, I tried talking to her, but that didn't work. I gave her little gifts without success. All I did manage to do was scare her off. I followed her home. Actually, it was more like chasing her. Then I started to have nightmares and dreams about her. She and I were lovers and she would get strangled over and over again in my fantasy. I was mad for her and couldn't stop looking at her. I needed her and I loved her right up until the end of the school year.

That year one of the new students at the school was constantly on my back, day after day. I got tired of it, lost my temper, and started to swing at him. I grabbed his hair and pulled. Then the teacher came up from behind me and yanked me away from him. A fistful of hair came out in my hand, leaving the kid with a bald spot. I was sent to the office. But he got to talk to the principal after I did. He cried and carried on and put on quite an act.

I'm sure he didn't tell the dumb nun about the things he had been saying to me all year and about how he had been harassing me. I'm sure he didn't tell her that it was the teacher's yanking me that caused his hair to be ripped out. Nobody told the nun about him. But I told her how he went around starting fights and even gave some kids black eyes.

I was almost expelled from school along with about forty others. The principal showed me a list of children who were being expelled from school and told me I might be one of them. So I had to stay after school and apologize to the jerk and the teacher. The teacher I did sincerely apologize to, but I was as cold as possible with the jerk who lost his hair.

The nun gave me the handful of hair and told me to go home and tell my mom what had happened. To prove that I had told my mother and had shown her the hair, I was supposed to ask her to write a note and to tape the hair to it. So I went home and confessed the whole incident to my mother. To my surprise my mom sided with me! She wrote a note to the principal who read it and was satisfied with it. The note read, "He has told me what he did and we shall take care of it." I became infamous among the students and teachers because of this incident for the rest of my high-school years.

In eighth grade, in the drama club, I tried to get a play going, but I was never allowed to. Besides, the eighth-grade teacher was doing plays with the four upper grades. So I guess the school had enough stage material to last a lifetime.

9

A Reputation to Haunt Me

The Lunch Bag

Eighth grade was the worst school year of my life. The things I did in this year would be remembered, talked about, asked about, made fun of, and judged by everyone until grade twelve. My humiliation and embarrassment made better entertainment and was funnier to the kids at school than any movie or play. In fact, it might as well have been a show on stage because the whole school saw it. It made local juvenile history and was in the juvenile gossip grapevine. It could have been titled "The Hoods, the Jocks, and the Innocent."

My first name became connected with the bad reputation that I obtained and with the incidents that would haunt me for the rest of my school years. From here on, people would expect me to do the same, just for the fun of it, and all in the name of entertainment, and there was nothing I could do about it.

I was eating lunch in the gym with the rest of the students when a bag fell into my lunch. I thought some wise guy had tossed an empty bag at me, so I threw it in the garbage. I did not realize that somebody's lunch was inside. The lunch belonged to a guy whose sister I was in love with; I had had a run-in with him the previous summer. When he saw what I had done to his lunch, he took my lunch and smashed it all up. I flew into a rage. All the years of school seemed like a prison, and I was tired of being the butt of everyone's jokes. Since everyone already thought I was a monster, I decided to live up to the reputation I had.

I chased him all around the gym in front of everyone, and when I caught him, I started swinging like a madman at him. As usual other boys grabbed me by the arms and tried to restrain me. But I fought them off until they had a good hold of me. Finally, the principal, who was a nun, told them to let me go. When they did, I was struggling so hard and was so angry that I spun away from them and accidentally slammed into the nun.

As punishment, I was forced to sit in a storage room of the gym with the door opened so that everyone could see me as they walked back to their classes. Everyone going by looked at me, and some thought the whole thing funny.

After lunch period, I was told I had to apologize to the whole school. So I spent that entire afternoon going from one room to another apologizing to every teacher and student for my behavior. I must have said I'm sorry to over four hundred students and teachers, even though I was not sorry at all. I was being displayed as the worst-behaving student in the school's history. This was brought up to me every now and then for the rest of my school days.

A counseling center was the next thing my mother tried. At first, the counselors tried to act as referees between home and school. Then they started in on family matters and just let the school off the hook. That turned my mom off, and before long she put an end to my counseling sessions.

The Stare

During the summer before eighth grade, I fell in love with a girl in the seventh grade who was new to the school. She was very nice to me at first, and said hi to me every day. I said hi back and soon made it a point to greet her every time I saw her outside at recess and in the halls when we switched classes. But it didn't last. When I started giving her gifts and talking to her, she quickly developed a profound fear of me and wouldn't have anything to do with me. After a while, she ignored me totally.

This change shattered me. It might have been the result of people making fun of her for being friendly to me. I tried to win her back but, of course, I failed. She couldn't have cared less about me, and it made me angry. Out of spite, I started following her everywhere she went. I would stare at her at lunch, outside at recess, and when we switched classes. I knew it bothered her and I did it just to make her mad. But I would have stared at her, anyway, because to me she was the most beautiful thing in the whole school.

My lust and frustration soon grew into a madness which I could not cope with, and it went on day after day. Although I tried everything I could think of, she wouldn't speak to me any more. It was hopeless, and it wasn't fair because she had started saying hi to me in the first place. At night I cried and then I masturbated with her in my fantasies. Like all the women in my fantasies, she was strangled to death. But I couldn't get enough of her. She had to be in every fantasy. During the day, I had to stare and stare, and I didn't care what people said about it. I thought she was mine. I wanted and needed her. I just didn't have any other friends whom I could talk to and be comfortable with. There wasn't a soul in the universe whom I could go talk to about my feelings. The whole situation was a joke to others. They would just laugh at what I was going through.

Of course, I was in the wrong. I am always wrong about everything. I have been ever since I was four years old. So why should this have been any different? Any friendship I ever had with a girl went sour or ended for some reason. She would drown or move away, or I wouldn't be allowed to play with her. I'm always in the wrong.

My lust for her grew into a disease or an addiction which I just couldn't get away from. I really had no control over it. Her hips drove me crazy. I couldn't escape her eyes. Her tiny little breasts turned me on and so did her hair. I wanted to put my tongue in her mouth. Her butt would give me an erection and I would feel like I had to have her. But I never did. She was the first girl whose clothes made an impression on me. I remembered every thing she ever wore. Her black pants and black nylon shirt with gold flowers were my favorites.

The guy whose hair I had pulled out started to tease me when he discovered that I liked her. He thought it was a big joke. Even though I had pulled his hair out, he said he could get me a picture of her if I paid him five dollars. He said that it would be a 5" by 7". I told him I could only scrape together three bucks, so he gave me a wallet-size picture of her instead. It turned out that he didn't have a 5" by 7" picture, so I was glad I hadn't given him five dollars. Of course I was happy to have the picture—for all the good it did.

There was another unbelievable beauty at school who was a grade behind me. I did not realize it at the time, but I was to have a mad crush on her in the future. In three years I would be lusting for her long brown hair, brown eyes, and her classy Irish looks. She had a great body, and she was shorter than the other eighth-grade girl I had the crush on now. She also had the saddest, prettiest face and expression I ever saw. When she smiled it was like a rainbow. So actually I had her in my fantasies from the eighth grade, but my lust for her started in eleventh grade. I called her the "Quiet One."

Horror Movies

The old Frankenstein, Dracula, Wolfman, and Mummy movies were favorites of my nieces and me. I used to pretend that I was the mummy and each of them would take turns being carried off by me. It was really easy to pick them up, even when they went limp as if they were dead. We held seances, pretended that we could talk to the dead, played "ghost of the graveyard," and tried to read minds and lift things up in the air by telekinesis.

When we were not together, the youngest one, Kim, and I used to write letters to each other. One time we sent a cassette tape with messages on it back and forth through the mail to each other. We carried on as if we were in a cult.

Alfred Hitchcock movies were a big thing with us too. We used to sit and talk about the shower scene in *Psycho.* I played the death scene over and over in my mind like a constantly repeating tape. Then I taped it on my little tape recorder and played the audio over and over again, while in my mind whomever I had a crush on was in the shower getting knifed. I did that a lot with television shows too. I taped the soundtracks and then went into a trance, playing the show in my mind with my own actors selected of course from school.

In a sense I was directing the show in my mind as the audio tape played on. I did this type of stuff all the way up to twelfth grade. Then I didn't do it with television shows any more. Instead I used music from the radio or from movie soundtracks. As I listened to the music, I would make a mental tape of a movie—and they weren't too bad. If only I had millions of dollars, I could make my own movie and direct it for real.

"Dark Shadows" Girl

I almost forgot to mention, or maybe I've avoided mentioning, that in eighth grade there was another girl whom I had been in love with, from the first grade, when she was so tiny it was beautiful. She had blonde hair and blue or brown eyes. She is the only one whose eyes I forget.

I never could play with her because she avoided me as much as possible, but I think it was because of the other children's teasing. The whole class knew I liked her. She would talk to me in secret but not in front of people. She was the sweetest of all the girls. One time she gave me this toy ring that you put on your finger like a real ring. She gave it to me because it was similar to the type worn on "Dark Shadows," the television serial I liked.

She lived right across the street from the school. Her big brother used to give me a rough time because he knew I liked his tiny sister. He had to be the fattest kid in school. But he didn't bother me for too long because he turned out to be a nicer guy than I was led to believe at first.

By eighth grade she had a fantastic figure. She was quite full and looked cuddly and squeezably soft. She wasn't fat, but at five feet her body was quite filled out, like the ones you see in the girly magazines. She would have been called well developed. In eighth grade I imagined her being drowned or crushed by something, and at the point of ejaculation I would imagine her vomiting blood. This new type of fantasy death I discovered in the horror movies that were rerun on the Saturday-night horror show.

I'm told that it's normal for boys to chase after girls, but I wonder if my problem is girl-mania or something. I really like girls but no matter how careful I am with them, even if they don't know about my fantasies and I don't stare, they still don't like me. They end up going out with a football, basketball, baseball, or swimming champ. I've never been like the rest of the boys. I was always weird and always making a fool of myself. I spent most of eighth grade staring at the girls from school and masturbating while having fantasies about them being strangled or drowned.

10

Poems of Love Unattainable

Her-She-Girl

Her hair was long and dark
Her eyes were blue
At first she always said hi to me
And I said hi to her
She said hey man
I said you're nice

She wore a white tennis dress
When she played tennis and beat me
She played ping pong and beat me
I fell in love with her and she wouldn't play
This was in the summertime

I gave her sweet things to eat
I followed her wherever she went
I talked to her all the time
She got sick of me
And this was in the fall

She wore black slacks which drove me mad
Her black shirt was a slippery nylon
With gold flowers on it
Her-she-girl

My first stare
My next stare
I could not get her out of me
I could not stop loving her

I wanted this girl for me to keep
I cried at night
I stared in the day
Following her everywhere
If she would only talk to me
But she stopped long ago by now
It's almost winter

I wouldn't have stared so hard
If she hadn't stopped talking to me
But she said it and it hurt
I hate him, she would say
It shattered my heart
I will never look at her again
But I couldn't stop
I was mad for her

She wore light green slacks and a reddish sweater
I was obsessed with her body
I wanted to touch her and cuddle her
Day by day it got worse and worse
One day she wore all black
In the front of her shirt
Was a large red stripe
Month after month I was insane for her
There wasn't a moment I wasn't thinking of her

I saw her in the mirror
I saw her on the wall
I saw her on television
I saw her in the window

I dreamed of her constantly
I undressed her in my mind
I loved her waist
It looked so smooth and curved so nice
Her breasts were beautiful
I loved the way she laughed
Her smile was so exciting

Obsessed, obsessed, I lust, I lust
Every night over and over

Her in every climax
Madness of obsession
I cry I want her
I want, I want, I want
Insane
I chase her and stare and
Stare and stare
I won't do it again
I won't, I won't
When I see her
I flip, I flip

If only she would love me
If only she cared
Of course the whole school knew about it
Embarrassing and humiliating
But all my life it happened to me
So I was used to it
But she was not
Madness madness
I wanted to live with her
I couldn't concentrate on anything except on her
Her buttocks her stomach her pelvis and crotch
Her lips her legs her belly button and waist
Nightmare, nightmare it won't stop
It won't stop
I couldn't stop, I was ill and sick
No one to run to and no place to get help
For she was my fixation and I couldn't stop

From the month of June
To the month of June
A whole year of this
It's too much
I want to die
I cannot stand it any more
I love her, I love her
Madness and lust
Lust and lust and lust and lust
Climaxing over and over night after night
No stopping
It's always her image

I want, I want, I want
No end to it all
No end
Fights at school
Swearing everywhere
Depressed at one time
Dying of laughter the next
Crying at night
Staring by day
One last cry for her
Then the miracle came
She moved
She moved far away
Slowly she faded from my brain
It took three more months after June
To finally break free of
Her-she-girl

Stare, Stare, Stare

To stare is a curse for I cannot stop
I stare to love to look and to hold
But these will never happen
Instead I stare girls to death
I stare because they are beautiful
Madonnas to be
They are untouchable and too important for me
I can only love one kind of girl
I cannot escape it no matter how hard I try
The girl must have brown hair and brown eyes
Brown is in the fantasies that invade my sleep
I get no sleep because I am obsessed
With brown hair and brown eyes
In every case the hair is long
And she is beautiful and sexy and soft
Soft and cuddly and smooth and scented
I want, I want, I want
But can never have
For she is terrified and vomits at the sight of me
I cannot talk to girls because my presence humiliates
They will be made fun of

And spat on for being seen with me
I am a creature and not a human being
My IQ is below average and I do not meet the standards
Of supermen who will possess her
And take her from me
But people cannot understand the problem I have
Even if I did not stare they would run away from me
My eyes pierce
People think I am weird
There is no help for me no matter who I tell
They just say I should stop
That is impossible
The girl I want I must have
I lust and love and go crazy to have her
My fantasies go crazy and beyond the norm
For I am a paraphiliac and there is no place for me
The doctors and counselors have no help for me
I cannot get help because I am the only one like me
I can only love by my own punishment
I can only choke myself
I choke for love and get punished at the same time
I choke for lust and love and the girl that is never mine
Paraphilia runs its course
All the way to the end of life
And when that happens I am a corpse

The Epileptic Girl

She had brown hair and brown eyes
She was shy one minute and a pain in the next
But I was in love with her so many times

All I could think of was her nude body
I bet it was dynamite and full of ecstasy
She looked so cuddly and soft and sexy
But she was strong and tough yet a baby
She used to play with dolls and dress like a charmer
She dresses like a woman now
If only I could see all of her

She was great when you were alone with her
But dangerous when she was with others
She tormented other girls and made trouble for them
I didn't understand her when she was quiet and sad
I didn't understand her when she was loud and silly
I used to walk home with her when she would let me
I don't know why she showed me the inside of her house
I don't know why she talked to me at all
I don't know why she talked against me before that
But I wanted her so bad and I wish I knew why
I was madly in love with her and I wanted to marry her
I was obsessed with her body every square inch

No one can love me for it is against nature
It is against nature for anyone to love me
No girl can love me for that ends in disaster
I loved her so much and she was so beautiful too
I wish I could have been a part of her and loved her
But what in hell for? She would cause me nothing but trouble
But whenever I heard her talk or laugh it drove me insane
And no one ever really knew of my madness for her
My madness for her buttocks and legs, eyes and hair,
Her breasts, her navel, pubic hair and vagina

I saw her cry once and I fell for her more
She was beautiful when she cried
And I found that she was human
For she was an epileptic and I wanted to save her
I wanted to save her from an epileptic seizure
Then after she came out of it and foam was on her mouth
I would grab hold of her and squeeze her in my arms
And tell her how much I loved her
And that I would care for her

I tried to get a teacher to play Cupid for me
But the teacher said
She is getting married
She would love to go out with you
But she just can't, she's in love with somebody else
I was shocked
For this is when I found out for the very first time
I bawled and sobbed and cried like I hadn't in years

The last time I cried was when she made fun of me
It was that incident that put me in
The Program for the Emotionally Disturbed
No one ever knew of my love for her
No one understood nor did I
For I had failed again but that was nothing new
Was she lying when she said she would go out with me
Or did she say that just to get rid of me
Or was she telling the truth?
I am so confused

She didn't love me. That is against my nature
Any girl I want never loves me back
I want the girl I love to love me back
But it is only a one-way street
I'm tired of assholes telling me that
It has to be a two-way street for love like that
I think to myself
What a bunch of stupid assholes
Now tell me something
That I don't already know

"Dark Shadows" Madness

Victoria Vanity Virgin
Maggie Madeira
Carolyn Captivate Climax
Sarah Sad Seductive
Angelique Addictive
Victoria Victoria Lust Lust
Maggie quiet shy sad and unhappy and more lust
Carolyn a nun
Sarah Sadistic Lust
Angelique Climax Climax

As we lust we hate and we are
All mad to the extent of our
Exhausting lust needs
Dark Shadows is like a light source that
Puts me into the recurring fugue and
Never ending obsession—so Collinswood

Becomes the house of the madonna
The whore and the lust of it all
The men are nowhere in sight
The fantasy is of the females of the fugue
Men are the symbols
The women are the centers
Of all things to the end

Ellen

Ellen is she
She likes to dance
Dance in aerobics
For she is hooked
Hooked on aerobics
Like the rest of me
I watch her
During her dances
When she says things like
Come on now, don't stop, keep going
She shows everybody how to dance
But I don't dance
Because I'm in a staring trance
For I love her too
She is a Replica
She like so many
So like the ones before
For I am there
To stare at her again
Only she can't see me
So she won't get scared

Scared of my unreal stare
As others were
Others from before

I turn on her program
Every single day
To watch her beautiful self
Dance all day
But it only lasts half an hour

The show is over then
But her image lingers on and on
In my brain all day
For I was addicted to her
Again and again
Watching her long brown hair
So long and dark
In a pony tail
It bounces so nice
It swings back and forth
While she dances
And leads the show on
People are supposed to do
What she does on the show
But I am unable
I'm watching Ellen move

But she is safe
Safe from my stare
She lives a long ways away
Away from my love
And any added embarrassment
She is safe
I am safe
I try not to watch her any more
I go for weeks without her
But I might think about her
And that hunger is there again
Then I must watch her
Just once more
Then I stop for a few days
Then I'm lonely again
I watch her all over again

Ellen Ellen
I need you so
For I only know
I am addicted to you
To watch you bounce like you do
For I am mad
And you are voluptuous
I love every part of you

And when you say things like
Don't stop, slow down easy
Then it gets sad
You are going to leave
Until the next time
That time may never come
The show may be cancelled
Or you won't be there
The way you look into the camera
With those big brown eyes
I wish
You were mine
Ellen
I wish you were mine.

Peanuts She Is

She is so sweet
She is so nice
She is so quiet
So lady-like
So articulate
So cute
So well mannered
Peanuts she is

I could never get enough of her
I was addicted to her
Like peanuts
I could eat and eat them
And never stop
Peanuts she is

Peanut butter reminds me of her
Whenever I think of her
Peanuts
I see her again and I thought of it again
Peanuts
She acted like a peanut
She was a peanut

Of course her hair was brown
Brown eyes too
It hardly ever fails
Peanuts she is

She never was afraid of my stare
She never said anything against me
She never tormented me
She was always sweet to everyone
But she was so quiet mannered
But somehow not shy
You could talk about anything with her
She never dressed fancy
She dressed neat
My favorite was her pink slacks
With her pink slippery jacket
That was only waist high
That was the loudest thing she ever wore
Some blue jeans here
Dark cords there
Even after we graduated from school
She still didn't hate me

At least I don't think she did
She was cool
Peanuts she is

11

Homosexual Strangler

Was I Turning into a Homosexual?

In ninth and tenth grade, I was still crazy about brown-haired girls, never blondes or redheads, only brunettes. I usually masturbated twice a day. Sometimes I would go to six times in one day and maybe three times on another. Once I did it twelve times. I fell in love once per year with a girl I would be crazy about. As always I would get shafted. I didn't seem to match the muscle man, the type that girls I wanted went out with.

I began to hate falling in love. I even hated the word "love." I saw other boys and girls in school kissing and touching each other, and it began to make me angry because the girls would never touch me. Boys would tell me to just get a girl. But I never understood how that worked so fast and easy for them. Talking to them didn't get me anywhere. So I just stared and got tired of being turned down.

The school psychologist told me that my test results were in the range of someone who is educable retarded. The written report that they always read back to me was so negative that it only confirmed what I had always been taught about myself: that there is something wrong with me.

I used to have a horrible feeling that I was turning into a homosexual because I was a masturbator. No one in my family knew about it. They were convinced that I was morally clean and untouched by sexual appetite and sinful passions. I learned how homosexuals fucked before I knew how men and women fucked. I didn't really know how a baby was made until tenth grade. As a result, in tenth grade, I masturbated for the first time with fucking in the fantasy. But it was a fantasy of boys whom I knew in school fucking me. I would imagine that they would gang up on me, rape me, and then would strangle me. One would strangle me with his bare hands and two others would hold down my arms so I couldn't fight back. Another one would be on his knees playing with my sex organ. Then they would pull me into a standing position with my pants and underwear down. The orgasm came when I was strangled to death.

In another fantasy I was thrown into the school swimming pool. I drowned but my eyes were still open, and I floated to the bottom of the pool. Even though I was dead, I was able to see. I watched all the boys' naked butts and penises and concentrated on their pubic hair, especially the color of the hair around their penises and on their chests.

I was utterly obsessed with becoming a homosexual, while at the same time I was still falling in love with girls. When I wore tight nylon blue pajamas, I lusted in the mirror for my own buttocks and penis. I would pretend I was fighting and struggling in front of the mirror while I imagined a homosexual lust murderer was strangling me—someone like John Wayne Gacey. But it was not him exactly; it was someone taller than me, and he would be strangling me by hand.

The Mirror Strangler

Later I would use a miniature knitted scarf that my niece Jenny had made for me. I began strangling myself with it in front of a mirror. As I struggled against the scarf, I would imagine that a homosexual killer was strangling me. I choked myself and then pretended that I fell to the floor dead. While on the floor, I would imagine that the killer pulled my pants down and then played with my hard penis, masturbating me. But, of course, I was the one masturbating.

At other times in my imagery a girl got strangled or drowned. The orgasm came when there was an imagined death. Then I would come out of the trance, get off the floor, tired, and wonder why I did this thing to myself. I knew that it was not normal and I hoped that no one would find out about it. They never did and so I said to myself, "This is the last time I'm going to do this. I will never do it again. Never." But days or weeks or even a month later, the head rush would hit again: I smelled something burning and I felt pressure on my temples and butterflies in my stomach. The noises in my head increased—it sounded like hail raining on fiberglas—and the feeling of a sexual high became very strong and hard to resist. I would go crazy, slip on a tight pair of men's bikini underwear, and put the dance tights around my neck. I couldn't breathe but the thrill and excitement was just too much, and I couldn't stop. I strangled in front of the mirror, my beautiful butt and legs struggling and kicking and my face turning red until I couldn't hold my breath any more, and I fell to the ground. Finally after the murderer (me) masturbated my penis, I put the underwear and dance tights away in a special place and would sit and wonder why I do it.

In eleventh grade I was in school for no more than four hours a day. I would go home and masturbate about three times a day. Usually, my fantasies centered on some girl whom I had seen in school; she was usually being strangled. I choked myself with the scarf, but only in a very superficial way. I hardly tightened it around my neck when I first started. As time went by, I gradually started to pull harder. Soon I was really choking myself.

In many of my masturbation fantasies I was a disco dancer like John Travolta (whom I hate) from *Saturday Night Fever*. I imagined that I was wearing a tight, white jumper suit that sparkled in the lights while I danced. After I had danced, I would walk home at night, still wearing the suit. Suddenly, a bunch of boys would gang up on me and strangle me. My penis could be seen through the tight suit, and my pelvis struggled until the orgasm came with my last gasp. My mouth was wide open and my tongue stuck way out until it folded back in and disappeared when I died. The boys would just leave me there. My clothes were never taken off. I started using the tongue trick when I really choked myself in front of the mirror.

Ever since I began to masturbate, years ago, I thought that masturbation would turn me into a homosexual and there was nothing I could do about it. That idea was put into my head by the book about youth from Jehovah's Witnesses, which my brother had given me. I became obsessed by this notion and couldn't stop looking at teenage boys: thousands of butts, penises, and pubic hair. I used to get gas on my stomach from all of my looking.

At night I would have really vivid dreams of being choked or hanged while wearing my tight, blue, 100-percent nylon leotards. In these dreams I fucked men and they fucked me and then I got strangled. All I could see in my dreams was penis after penis over and over again.

The Hangman's Noose

In twelfth grade there was a huge shift in my path that I did not expect to happen. I got into another work program, this time working with exceptional children. I was soon to find out that other kids were getting shafted just the way I had been. I saw how they were treated and then I began to realize that what happened to me was happening to other children similar to me, and right before my eyes. I decided I wanted to work with children.

That soon fell through because it is a woman-dominated field, and they tore me to pieces because of "my underdeveloped social skills" with my so-called coworkers. They didn't like it that I enjoyed playing with the children. They thought I should act like a man, adopt an air of importance, supervise and watch the children, and set a good example for them. I was not supposed to get involved with them personally. So that took care of that. I ended up getting railroaded into day care centers and that was not what I had in mind.

That year I started to experiment more with my body. I continued to use the nylon pajamas resembling dance tights, but now I pulled them up so the material would be touching my chest. Then I would take a belt and tie it around my waist so that the nylon pants would be tight and my ass and legs could be seen through the material. I put on a root-beer colored dress shirt and the light-beige vest from my three-piece suit. I wore the vest over the shirt so the hip part of the nylon pants couldn't be seen. My legs in the nylon pajamas were blue and the material was tight on my skin, almost to the point of ripping, so that my butt was beautifully rounded. I had the look of a ballet dancer, like I was back at my family's old dance school.

Once dressed, I would take out a tape player and record my choking sounds on it while I struggled in front of the mirror. This would give me a throbbing hard on. As I played back the tape, I got even more aroused. I'd lay down on the bed, masturbating while I fantasized getting strangled in my odd outfit.

Sometimes I would put aggressive movie music on the record player, turn it up to full blast, and choke myself in front of the mirror. Then I would tie myself up and pretend that I was being raped and strangled by a homosexual killer. Finally, I would masturbate with that same fantasy in my mind until the orgasm came.

I used to have dreams in which I was dressed in my tight blue nylon pajamas pants, brown shirt, and beige vest. In the beginning, I would be smoking a cigarette. Then a hangman's noose would come down from the ceiling, grab hold of my neck, and pull me up into the air as if the rope were connected to a pulley. I would struggle in mid-air and my beautiful buttocks and penis could be seen through my tights as my pelvis lurched madly. Soon I would strangle to death and at the final gasp, the orgasm would come. Finally, the hangman's noose lowered my dead, sexy body to the floor. My eyes were frozen open.

These images would give me a hard-on, and in the morning I would masturbate to the dream.

I used to tie myself to a big stuffed pillow and pretend that it was a homosexual killer. I would fight and struggle with it in front of the mirror. Then I would masturbate. I'd have dreams of being fucked and raped in the same vest-and-pants costume. This was my nighttime dream and my daytime fantasy. It got to the point where I couldn't wait to get home from school to do it again and again and again in front of the mirror. If I even looked at the vest, shirt, or pants I would feel compelled to go through the whole ritual again. This went on almost every day in grade twelve and the next year as well. It was my only excitement and my only means of entertainment. The vest, shirt, and pants became the trademark of my very disgusting existence.

I would go to school with gas on my stomach and there was no one I could go to for help. By now I had very little to do with my brother John because he had become one of the most respected field overseers for the Jehovah's Witnesses in this part of the state and probably the whole state. Along with these commitments, he was married and had a son. I could never go to him with a problem like this one. I mean, I was the only one in the world with this problem. Right?

12

Replicas

Longing for Love

The contradictory mixture of erotic obsession and the longing in vain for love is typical of a paraphilia. Nelson's desire to be loved and to care for another persists, unfulfilled. He yearns to control internal strife and to establish a pair-bonded connection with a lover. However, forming an intimate erotic relationship still has eluded him. There is something lacking which nonparaphilic people find incomprehensible. Evidence of this lack is poignantly expressed in the poems and narratives Nelson has written to the "replicas" who had obsessed him earlier in life.

Lucy, the Quiet One

For a while I didn't come across girls who were replicas of Peggy. The girls whom I was talking to and imagining in my masturbation fantasies were not the replica types. They did not have the same look that would drive me to addictive staring. Not until the winter was there yet again another replica. Her name was Lucy Hill, but I called her the Quiet One. She was a year younger than I am, and a grade behind me. I had seen her only once in the past two years. She came into the grocery store where I used to work on weekends. Now I began seeing her again and again in the school cafeteria during lunch. My madness was to take over. I don't know what it was, but somehow I was obsessed with the idea that she was saying things against me.

I went to Mrs. Brown, one of the guidance counselors, to tell her that I thought Lucy was saying or thinking things about me and about my behavior. There was nothing to go on; it was all in my imagination. I found myself increasingly obsessed with her and I didn't know why. Mrs. Brown knew Lucy and wanted to have her come to the office so the three of us could talk about it. I didn't want to do that because Lucy would not have understood.

I followed her in the hallway, I stared at her in the cafeteria, and this went on for days, weeks, and months, until the end of that school year. I could not seem to stop. I was madly in love with her. She had somehow taken the place of Judy, the former replica. Lucy had straight, long, brown hair, and brown eyes. She had tiny freckles under her eyes, like Judy had. Lucy was beautiful, too. She had this neat look in her eyes and her face. We never spoke to each other. She was the only replica that I never had a conversation with, and never will. I couldn't stand the pressure.

Lucy had two "body guards" with her all of the time. They were her girlfriends at school. A good portion of the school's population had learned that I was now staring at Lucy Hill, and the whole thing turned into a joke for everyone else. For me it was agony, and for Lucy it must have been humiliating. I masturbated over and over to her image. All I could think of was her, and yet we had no relationship at all. She is a mystery to me. She had the saddest face sometimes. She looked like she was going to cry.

I usually ate lunch in the cafeteria with guys who were in twelfth grade, a year ahead of me. Every one of them knew about my thing for Lucy. One time during a regular lunch table conversation, I got up and tried to go over to the table where Lucy was sitting with her two friends. The guys at the table saw me start to walk toward her, and they all began to hoot "Yeah!" and "Ooh" and "Ah." It sounded like half of the cafeteria went into momentary hysteria. I never got to the table where Lucy was because she ran out of the cafeteria, red-faced with embarrassment, and her two friends followed her. I blew it again!

I then went to my regular guidance counselor, Mr. Wright, whom I used to talk to a lot after I was put into classes for the emotionally disturbed. I told him about the uproar that broke out when I tried to talk to Lucy and that one of the guys in the cafeteria had even said to me, "Why don't you go talk to her?" I had to fall for it! Mr. Wright said that I would have done the same thing if I had been in that guy's place. That explanation was supposed to justify their actions. I somehow don't think I would have hooted and yelled like the other guys did. Maybe it was he who would have done the same thing that they did. I wonder if anyone would have done what I had been doing for years with one replica after another? I wanted Lucy. There wasn't much else to say; it was always the same thing.

At the beginning of the next year, Lucy and I were registered in the Black History class. The second day of class she brought in a class-change slip to take the class at a different time. I knew she was leaving because of me. The way she looked at me the first day of class when she saw me meant that she was not going to go through the same crap with me again. I told the teacher, Mr. Raford, that she left because of me and he said, "Oh, come on," jokingly, and I said, "No, it's true." "Really?" he said and that was that.

Sometimes I feel terrible about what I did to Lucy. If only she understood. If I could get her to forgive me. If she knew why I was the way I was. I couldn't help it, I didn't mean it, but I wanted her and I just had to stare, I had to.

The Quiet One

She had long brown hair and round brown eyes
And never said a word
She looked so dreamy; she looked so sad
Because she knew my stare and she knew I was mad
I wanted her so badly

I stared at her in the hallways
In the cafeteria and at her locker
For she was the quiet one who looked unhappy
Unhappy at my existence for I never quit
I was there everyday to stare again
I tried to stop; I told the counselor
But she didn't understand
So I just kept staring and staring more and more
Why did I care? It was such a lost cause
But I just had to look and wish she were mine

The whole school knew and thought it was a joke
But I didn't laugh, for it wasn't funny to me
Her girlfriends made it a game, but I hated to play
All I could do was look at the quiet one
She was only sad when I was around
When I saw her like that I wished I had drowned
No place to go and no one to tell
To try to get help so I could stop staring
For it was no fun but I still had to have her
She was in my sleep, she had entered my brain
My fantasies were out of control
I wished I was dead

The quiet one and I never spoke a single peep
It was all in my stare; that was message enough
She'll never know of my misery and torture
For I am in love with the quiet one

The Quiet One's Ghost

She haunts me when she is not there
Invades my sleep
And lives in my dreams
She stands alone away from me
I want to go to her
But something stops me
I don't dare
For she is the quiet one who looks so sad
And terrified of me so I must stand still

It is only a dream
The ghost of the quiet one
But terror strikes me when I see
This ghost so sad and pained
She is haunting and
Invading me
I cannot escape her punishment

A superman appears
He is tall, good looking
The man all women want
He is the best and I can not compare
He can do everything I can't
He kisses the quiet one on the lips
She kisses him back, and the two of them stare
Into each other's eyes
I watch them unable to move
Then he disappears and takes her with him

I was alone in the bomb-exploded school
The school was a shambles
The lockers had melted
Into a tangled mess
There were holes in the walls

The ceiling sagged
The auditorium had caved in
Water pipes had broken
Leaking on the floors
A piano had rotted
Like a piece of old fruit
The staircases were dangerous
Everything was warped
There were no more teachers
No more fools like me
Who stared at the quiet one

She haunts me now
But it's not really her
The ghost does it for her
I wake up in the morning and the dream is over
And I am in tears, for I lost her again
The one who was quiet and shy and unhappy
And now her ghost stalks for revenge

Daphne, Goddess

I first saw Daphne in twelfth grade and I immediately freaked out. She had very long dark hair that was nice and straight and the roundest blue eyes I ever saw. She was the tallest replica. I guess she was about 5 feet, 8 inches. I saw her in my acting class, which was full of beautiful women, but Daphne just had that look. She was popular. So I wasn't alone in seeing her beauty, but I was alone in the way I felt about her. No one felt about her the way I did, and no one else acted the way I did toward her. I tried very hard not to make a mess out of the situation by staring too much at her.

I tried to talk to her but I was not good at that. It took me a while to finally get up the nerve to talk to her. When I did, what was going on inside of me was unreal. My legs were like lead, but they somehow moved toward her. I had butterflies in my stomach. I felt weird and thought that something was burning because I could smell smoke, though I knew nothing was on fire. It took great effort but, unable to stop, I went over to her desk for the first time and sat in the empty desk in front of her. She was facing the other way talking to someone else. When she noticed me sitting there, she turned around. Then I simply told her that I didn't have a crush on her but I thought she was the prettiest girl in the school.

She responded, "Oh, thank you. That's sweet." And I said, "You're welcome." Then I got up and went back to my own seat at the side of the room. I was drained of energy and exhausted. She had such a beautiful face, such a beautiful everything. Her eyes penetrated me. She wore a black shirt and black pants, and had a white sweater over the shirt.

One night I had a vivid dream which seemed so real it was as if I was there. This "real-life" dream was of Daphne at age five. She was dead, and her naked, frozen body was standing in a large freezer. Her blue eyes were wide open and her hair was divided into two braids like pony tails. She had no breast development yet, but she did have black pubic hair at the appropriate place. She looked beautiful. That was the end of the dream.

I guess in the dream I was just standing there looking at her. Her image was very similar to the pregnant girl who is strangled at the end of the movie *Frankenstein: The True Story*. She is found outside, frozen in the snow and ice, with her blue eyes wide open. She had long black hair and was beautiful. The baby inside of her was dead.

At the beginning of every class, before the bell rang, I was the first in the class to see Daphne walk, run, dance, or fly into the room depending on how much time there was before the bell rang. She always managed to get there on time. She once had a black dress on that was made out of slippery nylon material with gold trimmings and gold cuffs. The dress was buttoned from the front and the gold trimmings were like flowers all over the dress. I had to say to her: "That's a pretty dress, Daphne." She said "Thank you," sort of embarrassed. I found that she had been a dancer since she was little. She appeared in the newspaper, modeling clothes. I cut them out and saved them. She had green pants on and a white shirt made from that slippery nylon material, with green flower-like trim. It was this shirt that made her breasts look so firm, perfectly formed, and beautiful.

My fantasies were going crazy as usual. She was strangled in most of them while I had an orgasm. In others, she was speared, and blood gushed out of her mouth before she died. In yet another, she put up a violent kicking struggle in the boy's locker room before she was finally strangled. It's always the same, it seems. I loved her. I wanted her. She was a goddess to me.

Whenever she came into the room, I always said, "Hi," and she said, "Hi," back. It got kind of comical because everyone knew I was looking at her all the time and they expected me to greet her.

At the end of the school year I was in a show called the Thespian Follies. It was like a variety show of music and comedy. I played Spock in a "Star Trek" comedy sketch from "Saturday Night Live." Daphne was in a different part of the show where she did a jazz dance. She wore a green leotard dance costume which was skin tight. It ran from her feet to her shoulders, but on the upper part of her body was a vest made of shiny material which sparkled. She also wore an "I Dream of Jeannie" hat. I watched her doing her routine during the dress rehearsal. She danced to the song "Fame" by Irene Cara and it was incredible. The sight of her filled me with lust and pleasure. Before the dress rehearsal and before she had her costume on, she was in jeans and a shirt and she had the Jeannie hat on. I said to her again "You're so pretty," and she said, "Thank you," again. It had become a habit.

When I graduated from high school, I got a yearbook. The next year I got one again because I knew Daphne would be in lots of the pictures. The next year she won the Miss Jonesville Pageant. She wore a tight, white wrap-around dress. I attended the contest, and after it was over, I went backstage and kissed her hand to congratulate her. After this experience, I freaked out for a week. I tried to get a tape of the show but they wouldn't give it to me. I cried for a week after the show and even wanted to make a mannequin of her. Then I wanted to make a three-foot doll of her called Daphne Doll, and I wrote a movie script called "Daphne Doll." I called around to factories to see if I could order a design for this doll. They told me I had the wrong place. I tried to locate the man who created the Barbie Doll, but he had an unlisted number and address. I went to many stores, looking for a gold bracelet and necklace like the ones Daphne wore when she won the Miss Jonesville Pageant.

I also attended the Miss Illinois Pageant. She lost and didn't get into the top ten finalists. I had pictures of her anyway. She wore a gold evening gown and looked like a being in a shrine of some kind.

After the Miss Illinois Pageant, I went to see her at the arts and crafts show which was set up to raise money for the next pageant in Jonesville. A week later, I went to see her at a show at one of the small malls in Jonesville called Fairfield. Her fiancé was with her and she was also with three other boys with whom she had graduated. They were all chatting with her. I didn't go near her, and she didn't wave to me although she knew I'd be there. She had colored her hair with a blonde tint that I hated, and there was no Daphne for me any more. She had had enough of me. The last time I saw her was at the Miss Jonesville Pageant, in which she gave a crown to the new Miss Jonesville.

I was crazy. I had gone this far, and was still addicted to the stare and to following her. Even after the first Miss Jonesville Pageant, I called the suicide hotline and got no help at all. I called the mental-health hotline, which is based on the top floor of the county mental hospital, and I got nothing from them either. They all thought I was calling them for attention.

Her street clothes drive me crazy
Her evening gowns kill me
Her dance costumes rip me apart
The tight green
The sparkled vest
The green "I Dream of Jeannie" hat
Her legs
Her calves
Her ass
Her firm breasts
Her everything
Mad for her
Crazy for her
Dream for her
Love her
Want her
Goddess

Her eyes are like oceans
I am drowning in them
Drowning to death
I am insane
Please somebody
Lock me away
Her slippery black nylon dress
With the gold flowers and trim
With the gold cuffs on the sleeves
Her pantyhose
Her green slacks
The white nylon shirt
Green flowers on it
Madness for her
Her black slacks, her black shirt
With the white sweater over it
Wanting her so bad
Love her
Want her
Goddess

I say to myself
I won't, I won't
I will not, I will not

But then when it comes to that time again
I end up in a trance
I cannot stop
There is no end
Only my suicide
Would put it at rest
What a way to live
What a slave I've become
If only people understood
Why I did things like this
If I could only be normal like everyone else
But I am not like that for I am abnormal
I will never be like other men
I cannot help it

I wish I had more pictures of her
But it would not help
Because I would never be satisfied
With whatever I got
So I would keep taking more and more pictures
And I would still not be satisfied
With what those pictures show
I cried, I cried
Every night for a week
There is no way a picture
Could ever give me what I want
And what I want
She would never give to me
So I could only mourn and grieve for me

Love her
Crazy for her
Obsessed with her
Mad for her
Lust for her
Insane for her
Love-mania for her
Die for her
Drown for her
Kill for her
Lie for her
Steal for her

Wish for her
Love her
Want her
Need her
Marry her
Goddess.

Replica Go Away

Replica, replica, go away, go away
I will not stare
Get away, get away
I will not love you
I will not follow you
I will not see you
I will not fall for you
I will not scare you
For I will leave
Wherever you are
I will not be there
Those round brown eyes
That long brown hair
That long pony tail
It isn't fair
That I have to care
For another
Another like you
For you are so beautiful
But that will not matter
For I am leaving you
Whoever you are
I don't even want to know your name
So please go away
But it will be me that will be away
So you won't have to see the likes of me
And then shudder at me
In your disgust of me

Part Three

College Years and Young Adulthood

13

Water Angel

Recapturing lost memories is like finding lost pieces of oneself and patching up the holes that the missing pieces created. The present can't be understood without knowing what once happened. There is a satisfaction in being able to cross the bridge from the past to the present. It is almost the satisfaction of being able to explain not simply before-and-after, but cause-and-effect. After years of total blackout, Nelson retrieved the lost memory of his "Water Angel" who lost her breath by drowning. It was the first glimmering of understanding his fixation on strangulation and his compulsion to strangulate himself.

Cemetery

Perhaps the most significant thing that happened to me my first year in college was a strange dream I had. This dream was of a girl with long brown hair and brown eyes who was sitting on a log on a sandy beach. Behind her was a pond. She just sat on the log looking at me as if she were posing for a picture. Then the dream was over. When I woke up, the dream was fuzzy, but somehow I knew I should try to remember it. There was something about the girl in the dream. Then it hit me—Peggy! Years after she had drowned in the pond, years after a total blank in my memory of her existence, I remembered.

I worked up the courage to go to the cemetery where Peggy, the girl who drowned hating me, the girl who caused the first smell of burning, was buried. I had never been to the cemetery before and I did not know where to find her grave. So the cemetery caretaker showed me a big map of the place and then drove out in his truck, and I followed in my car. When he left, there I was, standing all by myself looking at the tombstone of Peggy. It was the weirdest thing. I had made a discovery and it all made sense: all the drowning girls and strangling girls that I had seen on television were all her.

It was lonely there. I thought about the little tombstone. She lay six feet below me and I felt some weird feeling rush through me. It was as if she had told me to come. It was as if she had come in the dream to tell me that it was her, and to tell me to come to her. I talked to the tombstone but it was to her that I was really talking. I said then that I was sorry and I didn't mean it—I really didn't. Then I said, "I love you." I could never say that to her before she died.

I wished that all the replicas of Peggy understood, and I said to myself and to her at the tombstone, "If they only knew why I was so attracted to them—who they represented." All this madness, and yet I kept acting weird and couldn't stop. I was addicted to staring at them, scaring them, and teasing them, and I could not stop. I scared them the same way I had scared Peggy. If only I had known then what was really happening to me and why I was so obsessed with the brown hair and brown eyes. Peggy was my model. I had the same thrill and head rush with each of the replicas as I had with her. I just don't understand it. Standing there I said, "You probably cannot hear me, but if you do that's what happened. If I could just have been normal. To think what my brain was doing so many times over with other girls who looked like you, the same madness of wanting them but not having them, of staring and being unable to stop." I don't know how long I was there but I stared at the tombstone for a very long time. The wind was blowing. That was all that you could hear. It was so quiet and I was in some kind of trance.

The tombstone itself was just a little square block with her name and the verse on it. I went back home and then in a few minutes I returned to the cemetery with a double ceramic heart for Valentine's Day and my super-8mm camera. I shot some footage of the cemetery, the gravestone, and the joined double heart next to the stone. I thought that the shots I took might be good for a movie I wanted to make.

I wasn't able to give her any flowers before she died. She died hating me because I scared her. I don't even know why I scared her. The movie would be done for my school project in cinematography.

Water Angel's Movie

I wrote the script according to the newspaper article about her death. I took the view that her sister was not to blame for Water Angel's drowning. I wanted to make the movie not to pass judgment on anyone but because I was still in love with Water Angel and I didn't know why. The story is about obsession.

I was sure that she had brown hair and brown eyes, and to confirm this fact I sent out letters to the coroner, the courthouse, and the police station to get the reports on her. The reports stated clearly that her hair and eyes were brown. However, the paperwork that I got from the birth certificate, the coroner's report, and the police report did not give me enough information. I had no choice but to track down the family, which I didn't want to do.

In the beginning I had no luck locating the family since the girls had married and changed their names, and the one boy in the family wasn't listed in the phone book. Then I tried to track down the lifeguards who were at the pond when Water Angel drowned. I got hold of the mother of only one of them and she wouldn't give me her son's phone number. She was afraid that talking and being asked questions about something that he would rather forget would give him a nervous breakdown. His mother said that it was the sister's fault. I told her that laying blame was not the purpose of my movie. After this conversation, I felt discouraged about trying to contact more of the lifeguards. I knew that one of the female lifeguards, who was blonde, went into shock when Water Angel drowned. She probably wouldn't want to talk either.

I kept telling myself, "If only I had been there staring at her like I stared at all the other girls after that, maybe then she would not have drowned. If I had been there when she did drown, I would have experienced the impact of the tragedy too." As it was, I couldn't make a very accurate ending for the movie because all the reports had holes in them. Certain things did not add up.

For one thing the police report stated that Peggy's aunt was there and yet the newspaper article referred to the same woman as her sister. The police report also referred to a little brother, which didn't make any sense because she was the youngest in her family. There were other inconsistencies. The map that they sent me, which showed where her body was found, did not correlate with the rest of the report in the newspaper article. So I ended up with a story indicating that the oldest sister was at fault for Water Angel's drowning. That is not what I had expected.

Witnesses

The police report mentioned the name of the girl Lil who was with her and her sister when Water Angel drowned. I looked up the last name in the phone book but it was a common name with many listings. After making numerous phone calls, I finally found her and told her about the movie I was going to make. We had a lot of personal secret talk about

Water Angel which was important. She gave me the telephone number of Peggy's oldest sister, Mardy. She told me that I would have to call her to find out the details of the accident.

When I managed to contact Mardy, I learned from her that the drowning was very scary and horrible, and that Water Angel had been at the bottom of the pond for over forty minutes. The lifeguard found her through the use of scuba gear. She was caked with sand; her face was blue, almost black, from residue and lack of oxygen; and her body was like rubber. A female lifeguard had to be taken to the hospital for a while because she passed out.

I also discovered that the accident was not the sister's fault. She thought Water Angel had gotten out of the water to go to the playground, which was something she usually did. So Mardy looked for her all around the beach area not knowing that she was still in the water. When Water Angel did not appear during a rest period, she told the lifeguards, and then the beach was cleared and closed within five minutes.

A search party was quickly organized and a human chain was formed to walk through the water to see if someone could find Water Angel. They had no luck because they had to stop where the water was too deep to walk in. By this time the lifeguard whose mother I had talked to on the phone had gotten scuba gear. He went to the end of the pier and jumped off into the deep end. He wasn't under water more than two minutes when he came up with her. She was put on the beach and the rescue squad took over. They tried everything they could to get her to come back to life, but nothing happened.

Mardy told me that she had had to have psychiatric treatment and that every night she was tormented by a recurring nightmare. In the dream Water Angel came out of the water as if pushed by the force of the water which shot up like a volcano. She was full of waterweed and her eyes almost hung from their sockets. Her arms and legs were stretched out in a rigid pose. In a tone of reproach, she said to her sister: "I told you to watch me." It echoed on and on. Then she ceased being angry, turned around, and went back into the water. Everything calmed down again.

Mardy also told me about the funeral. She said that she went to pieces when a man walked up to Peggy's small white coffin. He stood there for a second and then opened her hand and placed a single yellow rose in it. She was buried in a yellow dress given to her by Mardy. Her mother could not be at the funeral because she herself was near death in the hospital.

After I heard all this and found out exactly what the swimsuit was like, I was sick to my stomach for the whole night, and in a depressed state. In the next two weeks I rewrote, for the third goddamn time, the final script. When I finished, I met Mardy at a restaurant and showed it to her. It was too difficult for her to read. She thought I was a nervous wreck, and she was right. I then made the mistake of saying that I could think of nothing but Water Angel, and that I had visions of her as an adult woman in the shower. Mardy said she didn't want me to make the movie if I was thinking of Water Angel in a sexual way. I told her that she didn't have to worry because the movie was geared toward kids, as all my movies are. She seemed to believe me.

Later I met Lil, the friend of Water Angel whom I had first contacted. She thought the movie was a neat idea, like Mardy did, and she gave me more information. She let me borrow the only picture she had of Water Angel, which I immediately copied.

Mardy thought that the idea of making this movie must have come from God through Water Angel who told me the idea in my sleep. I was flabbergasted. I had thought it was my idea from the beginning. She believed that after the movie was finished it would have some kind of message for the people who watched it. I hoped it would be a good message.

Water Angel's friend told me that she thought she could pray to her and ask her for help as if she were a real angel in heaven who knew everything going on in the planet. But I didn't really think that Water Angel gave me a message from heaven, because she didn't know me or remember me, nor did she want to remember me. I'm sure she died hating me or thinking that I was mean. How could she think anything else? After all, I was fighting with her, I had her by the arm and wrist, and she screamed. Although that's when I fell in love with her, she didn't know that. She didn't even know my name. She took off. I'm told she never liked boys, so that was probably due to me. How in hell would she give me the idea to make the movie? Why not give the message to her sister or friend, someone she knew and loved? I only knew her as a superficial image like all the other girls I've known and couldn't have.

Sometimes I wonder if I feel guilty for not getting to know her before she died. Maybe I feel guilty because I scared her and I couldn't say that I was sorry to her. She drowned not liking boys and that was because of me. I can never be comfortable with myself. It's thoughts like these that keep me awake at night. I seem to have deep depressing thoughts all the time. I'm never satisfied with what I say or do even though it may have been right all the time. I wouldn't know if I were wrong or right. It's the same to me and has been since I was five years old. I'm never sure about my competency, and sometimes I even test myself with the same problem to see if I am competent.

Deep inside me I know that Water Angel's sister and friend didn't like me because I acted strangely. I just don't have the personality to cut it with people. Her friend had a super personality and was 5 foot 10 inches tall with blondish brown hair and large beautiful green eyes. I wondered if I would have been better off doing all this by phone so they wouldn't have seen me. I always put on a lousy first impression. That's why I'm a friendless person. I don't have anyone. Why would anyone want to have anything to do with a freak like me? Knowing how I always mess things up, I was sure that with this movie project I would make more enemies than I already had.

I wish I could see Water Angel alive again, so I could say I was sorry for scaring her the way I did. I would also tell her that I'm not like the other boys, that I'm just a weird model, and the other boys are over six-feet tall and have muscles. I would tell her that I don't mean to scare people, but that somehow I just do. I wished I could talk to someone. I was just so lonely it was driving me nuts, and yet there were other times I would be glad to be alone.

Script

Before I even met Mardy, I had already cast the girl next door to play Water Angel, and her older sister to play Water Angel's friend. By some strange coincidence, the one playing the friend had the same hair, height, and eyes as the real friend. The girl whom I asked to play Water Angel looked like the real Peggy to me. She even acted like her. The two actresses are very beautiful girls, perhaps the most beautiful I have ever seen.

I originally intended to make a music video, but then I changed my mind and made a slower type of movie with longer shots. It lasted ten minutes. I got an A for it in the end. I paid none of the actors and got no money back, for I was unable to get it approved to air on television. Even if it had been aired, I still wouldn't have got any money from it. So I wound up in debt. The cost of the movie would have been pennies to a Hollywood producer, but it was enormous to me.

It is a very strange movie. The first scene shows some children riding bikes. On the front bike is the star of the movie, a girl about ten years old dressed in white with long brown hair and brown eyes. The scene quickly changes to a cemetery covered with snow. A boy, also about ten years old, is visiting the cemetery. It is windy and very cold there. He clears the snow away from the tombstone and places red plastic flowers next to it. Then he stands up and looks at the tombstone for a very long time. As he begins to think back in time, the film depicts what is going through his mind.

A gong sounds. He sees the girl from the first scene running from somebody. A letter saying "I love you" appears on the screen, followed by a quick shot of some flowers held in a hand. With that image we hear the sound of the gong again. He remembers more. We see him attempting to give yellow flowers to the girl but she runs away from him. He chases her but she runs too fast, and soon he gives up, turns around, and walks sadly away. She appears happy that she didn't get caught by him.

In the next scene she is walking down the sidewalk toward her house when she finds a letter stuck in the bushes. She picks it up and reads:. "I love you." She then looks scared and turns around to see if the boy is nearby. He is hiding behind the bushes but she does not see him. Frightened, she runs up the walkway to her house. The boy watches. Disappointed, he walks away slowly.

The next scene is by a river. The girl is walking downtown with two girlfriends and her older sister. Secretly, the boy follows her. She sees him and he waves to her. She takes one of her girlfriend's hands, pulls at it, and hurries her. The boy watches as they walk away from him. He is heartbroken, and looks down at the sidewalk. It's clear that she doesn't like him.

A squirt-gun fight at her house starts the next scene. Her two girlfriends squirt her, and then she retaliates, chasing them around a tree. They hide and she cannot find them. She looks around, puts the squirt gun in her mouth, and sucks the water out of it. Then, as if from nowhere, the boy comes from behind the tree. He has his own squirt gun and surprises her, squirting her in the face. She squirts back, but her gun is dry, so she runs to the front of the house to get protection from her older sister. But the older sister has made lemonade for everyone and motions the boy to come over for some too. She scowls, but they all wind up drinking lemonade.

The scene shifts to the present where the boy is at the tombstone still thinking of all this. But the gong bangs again and we flash to a totally unexpected scene. As the gong sounds over and over, we see a male lifeguard carrying the girl from the water to the beach to be given CPR. A female lifeguard joins him on the beach. He starts pumping on her chest while she does the mouth-to-mouth. The beach is empty. The sheriff is holding a hysterical older sister and preventing her and two friends from interfering with the lifeguards as they try to bring the drowned girl back to life. Two paramedics come with their equipment and try to resuscitate her. Then several beach personnel arrive and surround the girl and the paramedics. The gong keeps banging. The sister slips by the sheriff. A lifeguard tries to comfort her. As this hopeless scene drags on, it becomes clear that they will fail to bring her back.

Finally, we return to the cemetery where the boy is trying not to cry. He stands there for a long time; it seems like forever. The movie ends and the names of the actors and other credits are shown. There is no music in this film. Just the wind blowing from the cemetery. The gong stops at the end of the terrible beach scene.

I showed the film to the production manager at the nearest PBS station. After viewing it he asked me if my dissolves and fade-outs were done on the tape I showed him or at a film lab. I told him it was done at the lab. He seemed to like the movie. His first comment, however, was that it was primitive. I made it with a budget of $2000. That's cheap by any production standard. After six months the program manager's boss informed me that my film would be too strange for a PBS audience.

I know why he called it primitive. The mistakes could be noticed. But the story was strong and I thought it had a chance. My whole madness of the drowning girl and asphyxiophilia could have been my final project for any school anywhere.

Graveyard Poem:
The Flowers Are Waiting
For Peggy

The flowers are yellow
Others are orange
They grow in a flower bed
They watch everything
The flowers are waiting

They are waiting for the winter to come
When they will freeze and die
And after they die
All will be white
Until the next time
When it is warm again
When they are reborn again
To watch everything around them
They look sad, they look lonely
The flowers are waiting

They wait hoping for other things
To happen before winter
They wait for him
For him to come
For he will pick a whole bunch of them
And then he will take them to another place
Where does he take them?

Oh where, oh where?
The flowers are waiting

The orange flower said to the yellow flower
"When will he come? Do you think he'll pick me?"
"Pretty soon, pretty soon," said the yellow flower
"Remember last time when he picked a whole bunch of us?"
The orange flower asked
"Yes, I remember," the yellow flower answered
"He looked so sad"
"I wonder if he will pick me?" The orange one wondered
And the yellow one said, "We'll have to wait and see"
So they waited, soaking up the sun
And when it rained, they drank up the water
When the wind blew
They swayed back and forth
The wind would cool them
From the hot humid air
The flowers are waiting

Some flowers got old and withered away
Others grew in their place
Some people spat on them
And dogs would pee on them
And children trampled on them
Stamped them down, flattened, killed and buried them too
Once in a while a little girl would come
It would be the same little girl every time
She would come and pick a bunch of flowers
And then she would disappear until the next time
The flowers are waiting

And then it happened
He finally came
He looked so sad
He slowly looked about the flowers
He had scissors
One by one he cut the waiting flowers
Snip-snip-snip-snip
Away they went
Into his hand
He gently laid them side by side

He picked the orange one that likes to ask questions
He picked the yellow one who tries to answer them
He picked a whole bunch of flowers
He picked one that was the oldest, that might wither soon
He picked the one that was the farthest from the rest
It looked so lonely by itself
So he put it with the others
Then he gathered them into a bunch
He put them in his arms
And carried them to his car
He drove the car away and down the bay
The orange one asked
"Where are we going, I wonder, I wonder?"
"I have no idea, I have no idea,"
The yellow one said.
But they soon found out
They came to a cemetery

The car went through the cemetery
All the way to the back
There were thousands of tombstones
Big and small
Then the car stopped
And he opened the door
He picked up the flowers again
He picked them up gently
He put them in his arms again
And then he stepped out of the car
He walked over to a very small tombstone
And gently laid the flowers down
Down on the lower half of the stone
The whole bunch of them lay
Their stems on the ground
Their heads on the stone
He looked at the stone for a very long time
And before he left he said
"Peggy, I love you," tears running down his face
"I didn't mean it, I really didn't."

14

Asphyxiation Mania

Born to be Hated

In my first year of college I was tutored by some women who knew what they were doing. I found out from them that there was nothing wrong with me, but that the system was at fault. It was the system through which I had gotten messed up and ruined. The tutors told me that I could never get a full college education because I would have to go back to third grade. They didn't have any appropriate school program in college for me. But I kept trying.

Finally I dropped out of college because my self-strangling behavior was out of control. It came without warning, like a seizure. I was getting nowhere. I got no help from the suicide hotlines or from my counselor. I was tired of giving my family history. I moved to another city and went to another college.

I almost got railroaded into living on welfare and moving into a home for the mildly retarded because I lacked social skills and was a total recluse. I didn't have any friends at all. I would go to school and then head home to masturbate and choke myself. This is where my fantasies had brought me.

I was still choking myself to the point of almost collapsing. I used women's dance tights which I bought at a local department store. I was obsessed with men's bikini underwear too. All I could think of was the great feeling of wearing the tight bikini underwear and pretending that I had a homosexual lover. I continued to imagine that I was having a gay love affair and would fake intercourse in front of the mirror. The mirror was positioned in front of the bed where I was doing it. In the fantasy, the imaginary killer/lover would pick up the dance tights which were sitting in a pile next to us. He would yank them around my neck while I was french kissing him. I didn't suspect what he was up to; he made the blue nylon tights tighter and tighter until he was strangling me. I gasped "Shelby, Shelby! No, no, no! Why are you doing this to me? I love you!" But of course I couldn't say it clearly because I was choking myself to death. I would be lying on the bed naked except for the tight bikini underwear, gasping and struggling while watching myself in the mirror. When I couldn't stand the choking any more I stopped pulling the dance tights. I would have a head ache, my face would be red, and my neck had a red ring around it which would disappear shortly. Then I would masturbate using what I saw in the mirror as a fantasy. When I had the orgasm, I would finally be relieved.

After I was done, I would swear that I would never do it again. Then in a day or two, or even as long as a week or a month later, I would do it again, with the exact same detail. I could not stop. I had to do it, but I just couldn't figure out why. Before the madness came over me, I always experienced the same sensations: butterflies in my stomach, the smell of something burning, my heart and head pounding, hands shaking, pressure on my temples, a cold sweat, and the noises in my head growing louder. I could not escape. I could not escape! I had to close my wind pipe and see if I could scream, see if I could mimic the choking sounds of the women on television when they get strangled. I never got satisfied.

Sometimes the air seemed like jello which I couldn't seem to claw my way through. It was hard to walk from one part of the room to another. At other times, the air was more like water and it would be easier. Then all of sudden I'd get a burst of energy or emotion and I could fly through the air as if I had a rocket engine. But I'd tire quickly and the air would become like jello again.

The air smelled unhappy all the time. I didn't want to get up in the morning and wished I could sleep forever. I wished I had a girlfriend so I could have someone to talk to. I talked sharply to my mother and to my whole family all the time, and I didn't know why; it drove me nuts. Sometimes I couldn't love anyone. I wanted only to hate. At other times I wanted nothing more than to love and be loved. But I was not born for that. I am not the type that people like. I was born to be hated. People will never see me as anything other than weird. I have stomach aches all the time. I have dreams all the time about the lost loves that didn't love me.

I didn't know what to do. When I started to talk to counselors, I ended up exhausting both their listening skills and their interest in me, if there were any to begin with. This is because I talked and talked and never shut up. I never had enough social life and the opportunity to talk. Counselors wanted to send me away and put me in the psycho ward for an evaluation, or in a group home with a bunch of nervous wrecks to learn social skills. This didn't make any sense because I had trouble with people in the real world. Relating to other people with serious problems didn't help me to deal with people I met on the street and in everyday life. I had been in groups before and found them to be useless.

I can carry on a conversation and tell the whole group my secrets. I feel sorry for them, I baby them, and listen to them. I'm very receptive to other people's problems, but they're not receptive to my own. So the group home and the group discussions wouldn't work. I'm not trying to make excuses. But I know goddamn well what won't work, if I have done it before and have found it to be totally irrelevant to the situation that I am in.

I wish people and the professionals wouldn't keep labeling me as something that I am not. I'm sick of being categorized into a group of mixtures and so on. And I'll tell you this right now, if I'm put into a group, I know before going what will happen. It would be like the last time. I will fall in love with a girl there, and she won't have the least bit of interest in me because she'll have her own life to fix up. She'll be just as screwed up as I am. She would probably be married, have a boyfriend, be divorced, or have a bunch of kids. I'm really good at running into women who have children and are divorced, and that is not what I care to get into. Add to that the fact that divorced women are often ten years older than I am. I don't want to be raised by a girlfriend who will tell me the rules of things that you do and don't do when you are out in the world with a girl.

Sometimes it's as if the gravity on earth is as strong as the gravity on the planet Jupiter, and I've got a huge boulder on my shoulder and can't get up or move without a great deal of difficulty. It seems so tiring. Sometimes I can't stand to be with people. I want to be alone, but then I'm sick because I am alone, even though I wish I were alone. I wish I had somebody to love.

When I'm with people, I get myself so worked up and nervous that I end up saying the wrong thing and making a fool of myself. Then I hate myself and know that everybody thinks that I'm dumb, spoiled, ignorant, a dumb ignoramus, an idiot, a jerk, or a bullhead. I have been called all of these names by my mom, my stepdad, my sister, my nephew, and even my nieces who are my peers.

I've always been showered with toys, gifts, clothes, food, and money. You name it, I got it. But then people treated me as if they didn't like me. Although they took care of me, they acted as if I were in the way or something. So why am I not happy with myself?

I know the reason why. It should be fairly obvious by now. I hate living. No I love living. It's as if I just can't make up my mind. There is no happiness for me. I'm always love-starved, sex-starved, I can't get enough orgasms, or something else is bothering me. Even if a month or so goes by since the last time I choked myself, I know I will go back to it.

Television Drownings and Stranglings

Drownings of beautiful women on television turn me on. They put me on an emotional roller-coaster and I have to masturbate. The only way I can get the murder-drowning scene out of my mind is to tape the show on a video machine and play the scene over and over again until I get tired of it. Only then will my mind stop flashing the scene before my eyes. Television drownings are always sexy and glamorous-looking because of the scanty bikinis or swimsuits the victims wear. Stranglings of women on television also turn me on. I play these scenes over and over in my mind. Morning, noon, and night they play in my head. I can't escape them. I've also had a lot of homosexual fantasies in which I get strangled or drowned.

When I choke myself for real it is similar to the strangling on *Dial M for Murder,* and I do it in front of a mirror. The strangling scene in *Strangers on a Train* is my favorite. The first time I saw it, I got such an immediate erection that it hurt my crotch area. That was something. This scene recurs most often in my fantasies, except that I substitute any girl I want for the original actress. I imagined that scene over and over again in my mind for at least three years. I thought it was a sensuous and beautiful death. I've had an average of six orgasms a day. Since I was in fourth grade, I think that I have masturbated 12,000 times. I used a calculator to arrive at that figure. If I had or could have saved all my semen, I would have more semen than anyone ever had in history. I could sell my semen to thousands of women so they could have children without the men, and I would get rich.

Blood and Black Lace also contains a scene in which a beautiful woman is drowned in the bath tub. It shows close-ups of her under water, in detail. Sometimes I was obsessed with that fantasy too. She has only her underwear on and she dies with her eyes wide open. I have made up lots of my own murder fantasies, too. It would be great if I could make films of them. They'd be better than Hitchcock movies. They would scare some people to death and probably be a turn on for others. I'm sure my murders on film would be more frightening and sexier than any ever filmed before.

Another drowning like the one that I saw on *Blood and Black Lace* was on the "Charlie's Angels" series. The episode was called "The Killing Kind." It turned me on so much that it stayed in my fantasies for a long time. A beautiful girl in a red bikini is swimming in the ocean off the beach. A scuba diver comes underneath her, pulls her under, and drowns her. The camera focuses on her crotch and buttocks while she is struggling to get to the surface but finally she drowns.

When I missed a drowning on television, I'd go mad, cry my eyes out, and carry on like a fool. I had to have the tape so that I could watch it over and over until I got tired of it. If I saw a drowning scene on television and for some reason didn't tape it, I couldn't seem to get the scene out of my mind, nor could I stop masturbating at the same time. I'd have orgasm after orgasm, unable to get enough. After a couple of months, I would finally get over it. But if it were on tape, I would tire of it in only two days because I could play it over and over again.

With Intent to Kill was one of the movies that really upset me. I was cursed with it for four months. The night that I saw it I had at least seven orgasms in a row. The beautiful actress from the movie entered my fantasies. I was obsessed with the movie and I played the fight scene where she rolls over the dam again and again in my mind.

I had seen the coming attractions before the movie aired, but I figured they had set off a false alarm. They showed parts of the struggle that the girl had with her lover. I just didn't think the scene would have a great effect on me. When I watched the whole movie, I wished that I hadn't. I frantically combed through the television listings to find out when the movie would be rerun, so that I could tape it and get it out of my system forever.

I became so obsessed with the movie that I called the television station in town that carries CBS and asked when the movie would be on again. I was told that it would probably be aired next summer. I remember feeling shaky and excited while on the phone.

The movie wasn't shown again until three summers later. But I collected every *TV Guide* for three years because of it. I called again after the movie wasn't shown that next summer and was told that it would be shown the following year. I kept the movie review from the first time it aired and read it over and over again. I circled some of the words and then looked them up in the dictionary and circled them there. Anything said about the movie drove me crazy.

A Warehouse of Stranglings and Drownings

I was now strangling myself worse than ever. I was out of control. Sometimes I would even act out drownings. After *Blood and Black Lace*, I got into the tub with tight bikini underwear on and wore goggles that I bought for drowning. I had a mirror in the tub so I could see myself drown and struggle under the water. I imagined that I was tied down in the tub, face up, as the water filled up over the top of me. There was nothing in the world that mattered more to me at the time. The mirror was always aimed and ready, and I drowned myself over and over again.

I was freaking out: strangling myself in the middle of the night, masturbating six times in twenty-four hours, two or three times during the day and three or four throughout the night, sleeping in between orgasms, urinating all the time, thirsty all the time to the point of drinking three liters of soda a day, napping two hours every day after school. My memory was a warehouse of stranglings and drownings.

I went back into counseling but with a different counselor in a different county. The services were funded by the county because I was unable to pay the fees. For policy reasons, I had to go through another battery of tests to receive the funding. Many questions were like the ones asked by many others. More puzzles for me to do, more words to read, questions to answer, diagrams to draw. I refused to take the MMPI for the third time.

I was given a bunch of ink-blot pictures to look at. I was asked to tell the counselor what they were. Most were butterflies and bats with seminal vessels running down their middles, and they had vaginas on their groins.

I wanted to try hypnosis for the second time. I almost went into a subconscious state. I became very relaxed, but that was as far as I went. I could not be hypnotized. Counselors already had warned me before that it wasn't for me. I couldn't get any medicine to help me sleep, nor a shot to knock me out. But I was willing to try ANYTHING! Nothing worked. I was normal for a while and I thought that I would never ever do it again. BUT IT WOULD COME AGAIN. When I was doing it, it was the only thing in the world. I HAD TO DO IT.

The counselor sounded similar to all the others. He just said, "Don't do it." Don't I wish it was that easy? It was hell! But in the meantime I had established the link between Peggy and the replicas. Things were now making sense to me that I hadn't understood about my self and my behavior before.

I even tried to tell people on a mental health hotline about my whole autoerotic misadventures and my obsession with television murders. This didn't help because the women who answered the phone thought I was making passes at them, or that I was getting turned on by telling crank stories for attention. That has been really hard to live with. What good are the hotlines if they don't help people who are in trouble?

Orgasms

The orgasms that I have vary in intensity and length. I had a stricture of the urinary canal and was hospitalized to have it cut bigger so I could urinate better. After the operation, my penis was sore for a while, and

I had to wear a catheter. I soon found out that I could not go for very long without masturbating. When I masturbated, I felt a tickling sensation that I liked. When the orgasm occurred it hurt like hell during the first contraction, but after the semen started to come out the contractions were fantastically full of ecstasy. It stung at first. Then it felt really sensational.

It became interesting to me to have one orgasm after another. The first one had a lot of semen and was relaxing. If I had another one right after, it was even more sensual. The third in a row would be just as good as the second. With the fourth the penis began to get sore, and the semen was all emptied out.

If I had a bowel movement, then masturbated, the orgasm would be relaxing but not very sensually felt. But the second one right after that was excellent. When the penis was cold, the orgasm was not very good. When the weather was hot and humid, the orgasm was lousy unless I had been in an air-conditioned environment for a while.

After choking myself, I was full of tension. If I masturbated then, the orgasm seemed to be like magic, like lifting a boulder off my back. It was very relaxing. Sometimes I tightened the skin on my penis by pulling the penis out through the leg opening of one side of my underwear and making sure my testicles stayed on the opposite side, but still in my underwear.

The way I used to time my orgasms was like this. When I woke up in the morning, I masturbated to orgasm. When I came home from school, I'd have an orgasm, and when I went to bed I'd have another orgasm. If I was in the mood, which was usually the case, I'd have an orgasm before and after supper. On Saturday I'd masturbate when I woke up, around noon, once in the afternoon, once at supper time, again after supper, once in bed, and maybe again in the middle of the night. Always, always I had the image of a strangulation or drowning.

For a while my masturbation fantasies were focused on two lesbians. A blonde woman usually killed the brown-haired girl. Sometimes it was the other way around. The girl who drowned or strangled the other girl was my imagined lover. Then sometime later or in another fantasy she was killed either by me or by another girl. The star of this fantasy was usually Jodie Foster, who played the murderous lesbian, and the girl she killed was a girl that I knew or Melissa Gilbert or Melissa Sue Anderson. Sometimes the image in a fantasy was of a little girl who then became an adult woman, and when she was fully grown she was either the victim or the murderous lesbian.

Very rarely, but every now and then, my fantasy would be about a little boy who would be strangled by me or by a full grown woman. The boy was usually someone I had seen who I thought had a pretty look about him, girlish in a way without being a sissy. Of course there were always some fantasies with a homosexual feeling. I either got strangled or was drowned by another man who was usually bigger and taller than I was. He was someone whom I went to high school with, whom I knew by sight. In the fantasy I'd have gay sex relations in bed with him—getting fucked in the buttocks and mouth, everything—just before the murder occurred.

When I first began self-strangulation it was to the choking sounds of the movie *Frankenstein: The True Story.* I first saw that movie when I was twelve. It was an icky movie. At the end, the young bride of Doctor Frankenstein was strangled by the monster. She was about six-months pregnant and was wearing a blue evening gown, cut so low you could just see her breasts. When she was strangled by the monster she made some choking sounds that were classic. Since I first saw the movie, I have heard those sounds in my mind again and again in all kinds of strangling fantasies while I masturbated. In my fantasy the girl would also be pregnant, and I would hear the sounds she would make while being strangled.

Long before I self-strangled, I used to act out the sounds myself. In the Frankenstein fantasy, the choking sounds would happen along with my orgasm. I used to play the choking sounds over and over again in my mind hoping to get rid of them. When the movie reran, I taped it and I replayed the sound of her death about three thousand times on the audio tape player. In this way I finally got sick of it and eventually it didn't turn me on any more. I still have a tape of it, just in case I need to listen to it again.

I stayed fascinated by the sound of her choking voice. Her voice box was squished and you could just feel it yourself when she was choking. I would choke myself in front of the mirror with a scanty bikini on and would make the choking sounds from *Frankenstein: The True Story.* I did this over and over again and each time I would have an orgasm. I didn't know what was wrong with me. I needed it. And it seemed like it took forever until I was satisfied with getting the choking sounds to sound just like the ones in the movie.

Courtship Failures

I can't have any of the girls I'm attracted to, because none of them want to have anything to do with me or they already have a serious boyfriend. So my heart is always aching. I almost became involved with one girl. Then I found out she was a fundamentalist and went regularly to both Bible study and church. I would have had to be careful about what I believed in and what I said. I figured to hell with that. My life was already so restricted I was not going to get myself into that kind of trap.

Once in a while I would meet a girl who was really understanding and would think that I was a great guy. It always turned out that she was married or in love with someone else, so it would have been inappropriate for me to fall in love with her. It seems that any girl who is compatible with me will push me away. It always happens that way. One beautiful girl whom I went to school with was always running away and moving all over the country. Then when she came back home for a while, she wanted to do stuff with me. I was afraid to get involved because she always had plans to go away again. She just wanted to have fun, but I would have fallen in love with her just as she was ready to leave.

My mom and the girl's aunt, who are friends, set up a date for us. The girl's friends had all gone to college and she was very lonely, so they thought we should get together. She and I set up a lunch date, and I was very scared and uncomfortable all the way through the meal. I showed her some of the cartoons that I had made for children. After lunch, before she went home, she asked me to drop by one day. So I took her up on her offer and went to see her. She and her aunt both acted as if I wasn't supposed to be there.

All of a sudden my mom started talking against the two of them. For some reason my mom and the girl's aunt were not getting along any more. On the first date it seemed like all eyes were on us. Then, when it was over, my mom didn't seem to like the girl. It was confusing because one time she would say that I should go out with her and the next time she didn't like her. This kind of stuff has been confusing me since I was five. I could have said, "The hell with you," and gone out with her but then I would have fallen in love. It would have been impossible to love her because she was working two jobs and was going to move. In any case, I didn't have enough money to go out on dates because I didn't have a job even though I had applied. I just couldn't seem to do anything with ease and be comfortable with it.

Older Women

At the age of twenty-two I developed an attraction for women who were a good twenty years my senior. I had always liked attractive older women who held their age well and took care of themselves. They had to be well kept to star in one of my sex fantasies and they had to be beautiful. Often I would spot them because of their incredible bodies. Later, when I found out their age, I would be astounded.

I masturbated to images of these beautiful older women but in my mind they had special status because they were married already in real life and had children. I always pictured them as mature and highly intellectual people. In my fantasies they are not getting along with their husbands, so they seek me out because they know I love them and make them feel younger. We go to a hideaway somewhere and make love to each other. I use every sexual technique I know, and they are experienced and sexually fantastic. These women are always wearing pants suits or dresses that rich business women wear, and underneath great sexy underwear. After we make love, I strangle them.

Sometimes I imagine that they refuse sex because they change their minds, saying, "Oh this isn't right. I'm a married woman and have children." Then I strangle them. In another fantasy they have a heart attack, become short of breath, and finally suffocate while I watch not knowing how to save them. Then I have an orgasm. My heart attack fantasies make sense because they are older. It is easy for them to have a heart attack because they do aerobics all the time, which can bring on heart failure.

Sometimes I imagined one of them being drowned in a swimming pool by a girl who was jealous of her beauty. The murderer would be wearing scuba gear and would pull the beautiful older woman under by grabbing her feet. A great, sexually exciting struggle underwater would take place, until the victim couldn't hold her breath any more and drowned. I pictured bubbles coming out of her mouth and at that point I'd have an orgasm.

The rule for me was to focus on the girl's mouth and face when she made her final gasp as she was strangling or drowning. When I reached orgasm, I focused on her struggling legs, buttocks, or vaginal area, even though it was covered in a swimsuit, pants, or underwear. Other body parts that I normally focused on before the murder now came into focus at the point of greatest lust, the actual death.

My fantasies were always in serial form: the same one would be repeated over and over in my mind, and I would not be able to get away from it. It sometimes got to be a great mental strain. I would even dream about having a cigarette and then choking myself in front of the mirror in my tight bikini underwear. My subconscious mind never rested, even in my sleep. It was always tempting me to choke myself. The temptation to choke myself was there first thing in the morning right after I woke up. This happened far too many times to count.

When I was awake during the day I couldn't think of anything else but masturbation, orgasm, choking myself in the mirror, and an episode from some television show or movie which played over and over in my mind. It wouldn't stop until the drive had satisfied itself. It was as if the image in my mind had a power of its own, and sometimes I focused on nothing else but this mental tape. Once during a job interview, the image of a girl being strangled kept replaying in my mind, while I was listening to the employer. While he talked to me, all I could see was the murder in my mind over and over and over.

Television Infatuations

I had become an addicted erotic slave to the television screen. As soon as I saw a girl who was a replica of Peggy on television, the sudden madness would come over me: the burning smell, the pressure on the temples, the shaking hands, the butterflies in the stomach, the feeling of weakness and loss of power. My will was no longer my own. It seemed like some entity had control over me and I was pushed and driven by it. I didn't want to and I knew I must not tape the program. But I was unable to forget or to escape the television replica in my mind.

I'd focus on the clock, watching for the time when the show was scheduled to be on. I had to tape it. I lived in fear that something would go wrong with the tape machine. It became very important that there would be no interference from a storm or some other disturbance during the broadcasting of the program. Then I could get the best quality image. But at the last minute I'd have doubts and would say to myself, "I hope there is a power failure so the TV will go black. No, I must have it. I love her." My will swung back and forth like a pendulum. My obsession wouldn't leave me alone. It was always the same: the brown hair and the brown eyes, the image of Peggy, which never seemed to disappear.

If I had complained to someone about what programmers were putting on the screen, they would have questioned my sanity. "Just shut the TV off and don't watch it if it bothers you," they would have said. Then I'd feel worse and more addicted than I did before I made the complaint, as if the whole thing were my fault. Of course they didn't have any idea what I was suffering, and I didn't dare tell them for fear I would get in trouble for inappropriate comments.

It was mad, this infatuation for a girl whom I did not know and couldn't possibly meet. She might as well have lived in another world. I was totally helpless no matter what I did. The "help" I got did little good. "Just go for a walk or do some exercises" was suggested by one of the many professionals that I have consulted. When I did try one of those "not to think about it" techniques, it all got worse. The more I fought, the more dominant the television replica would become.

An excellent example of a television replica is Katarina Witt, the German figure skater. I had never watched figure skating in my life, let alone the Winter Olympics. But after seeing Katarina Witt the first time, I felt like I was tied to the chair and was forced to watch her by some outside force. Katarina is the replica on ice.

When the European figure skating championships were broadcast, one of the stations in my area carried the program live. I had the VCR hooked up and was ready to tape the show, when at the last minute, I realized that the television station had double-crossed me by broadcasting a local telethon instead. I surprised other people in the household when they heard a stream of obscenities coming out of my mouth. I fumbled around desperately with the VCR and the channel selector on the television attempting to find another channel that was broadcasting the skating. Luckily, I found one and was able to record the show. I probably missed only about a minute of the show, and it wasn't until later that Katarina Witt appeared. Then my eyes were like cameras themselves and I sat in a trance. After it was over, I was exhausted. I had a stomach ache, and I didn't feel very well because I was so upset and enraged at the station for preempting the show.

It was the same thing with other television replicas, like Samantha Smith. When she died, I had to tape every news broadcast of her because I knew they would show pictures and footage of her visit to Russia. When she died, I cried for her. Another replica was Angela Cartwright. I have all but four episodes on videotape of the *Lost in Space* series, in which she played Penny. In the three-year history of the show she wore four different costumes, and as a result there were four different Pennies in my fantasies of her.

15

Television Infatuation Poems

The Penny Fantasy
Dedicated to Angela Cartwright
of "Lost in Space"

All of my life
I have believed
That no one could ever love me
So how could one
So much more beautiful than I
Come even close to loving me
For you do not even know me
For you are my life-long fantasy
For I have loved you endlessly
The one so much more beautiful than I

Your brown eyes melt me
They soften my heart to sponge
A sponge that soaks
Every inch of your soul

I go mad
Every time I see you
I want to jump into the set
To be with you
To love you
Hold you
And kiss you too
The one so much more beautiful than I

It started when I was four
With your beautiful green dress
With the pink top
And the diamond shape on your chest
Your hair is so beautiful
It's dark and brown
It bounced as you moved
In your green tights and boots
Then I had a dream
Of you and me
We were playing together
In my little room—
How gigantic it seemed then—
And I thought of you
Every night after that
For I wanted to play with you
The one so much more beautiful than I

Then the show went into reruns
One after another
And I fell in love with you again
Only this time I was seven
And you were in red
Your hair was so long and beautiful
Your eyes just hypnotized me
Your voice
Your scream
Your everything hits me
I love you
I love you
So much
So much

But you're not really mine
For you're in the 2nd dimension
I'm in the 3rd
You are only touchable
When you're in my mind
The one so much more beautiful than I

Then when I was seventeen
I saw you again

They brought back the show
It went once more into reruns
And then I was in love with you
All over again
Just like when I was eleven
A never-ending fantasy
Over and over
I'm a teenager now
It's a whole lot different
Love after love
Fantasy after fantasy
A love that never ends
For the one so much more beautiful than I

Now that I'm twenty-one
In the video-tape era
I can watch you whenever I want
Tape every show that you were ever on
It actually took two or three years to do
From the *Sound of Music* to the *Celebrities:
Where are They Now?*
In my mind you will always be mine
The one so much more beautiful than ever now
So much more than I

Samantha's Serenity

Cheerful and calm and happy she was
Cheerful and calm and happy she is
She was before and she is now

My heart stabs with waves of pain
For the stolen Samantha in an invisible grave
The grave of peace and quiet serenity
The place where all of us will be eventually

Cry, cry, cry, cry for the hole in my heart
Good-bye, good-bye
Now only a memory
Just another page in history
The memory that will never fade

Samantha, Samantha I love you so
Come back, come back I don't want you to go
How silly that sounds
How my heart pounds
But I don't know how to stop myself

I see you in the paper, I flip, I flip
My heart flutters and shudders because I slipped
Into the trance of love and slavery
Slavery to capture every picture and book
Every video news and animated cartoons
Only because I love you

But you are safe from the agonies of the heart
You are with Him now and not with us
With us there's pain and sickness and betrayal
With Him there's peace and quiet
For me no calmness, no serenity

Revival of Samantha Feeling

Samantha, Samantha
Come back, come back
I lust, I lust
For you, for you
I want, I want
Only you

Your creamy skin
Your beautiful hair
That is so long and brown
And soft and cuddly too
Your blue eyes are so ocean-like
I'm drowning in them
Oh they hypnotize me
My eyes cannot stop looking in yours
So blue, so blue
I go crazy for you

Your smile is so bright
And rainbow-like

It causes butterflies
To swim in my stomach
I excite, I excite
For I love you

Earthspin

The 1984 Winter Olympics

I see her for the first time
I flip, I flip
Incredible madness
Lust
Obsession
Excitement
Explosions inside of me
She spins
She kicks
She dances
She slides
She skates
She laughs
She smiles
She is excited
She is happy
She has long brown hair
She has beautiful brown eyes
She has the earthspin
She spins the earth
The earth spins her
They both spin around the sun
The power, the intensity, the shocking beauty
Katarina Witt

The 1984 World Figure Skating Championships

Katarina, Katarina
Addiction, addiction,
Unable to stop looking at you
Can't stand missing you
Must watch you

Must videotape you
Earthspin

The 1985 European Figure Skating Championship

Cannot stop
Katarina
My pulse
My heart rate
It goes wild
Earthspin

1985 World Figure Skating Championship

Again and again
Unable to stop
Her lips
That skin
That smile
So bright like a rainbow
Earthspin

1986 European Figure Skating Championship

It hits again
Another head rush
Madness Earthspin

1986 World Figure Skating Championship

I'm loyal to her
I cannot leave her
Princess from within walls
Like the walls of my trap
Unable to escape it
She closes in all around me
Suffocating me
The Replica on Ice
Earthspin

1987 European Figure Skating Championship

Her legs
Her hair
Her ears
Her accent
Her laugh
Everything she wears
Again and again
Earthspin

1987 World Figure Skating Championship

Exhaustion
Tired
Loyal
Must watch
Must see her
Must tape her again
Cannot stop
Addiction
Earthspin

Epilogue

Katarina, Katarina
Like peaches and cream
A hunger for you
Like oranges and bananas
I flare for you

For she is the Earthspin
Who spins the Earth
The Replica on Ice
She slides
 She dances
  She smiles
   She's happy
    She's so she-like

Her lips
 Her nose
  Her eyes
   Her hair
    Her legs
     Her skin
      Her neck
       Her everything
        For she spins the earth
         Like the earth spins her
          And they both spin around the sun
           The power! The intensity! The shocking beauty!
           Katarina Witt
           Earthspin

Henrietta

Henrieta, Henrietta
I lust, I lust
For your beautiful hips drive my thrust

From the airwaves
I capture you, I capture you
And onto the television screen
And then into my heart
I go crazy with love
I stare in a trance
Butterflies dance
Dance in my tummy
My brain feels funny
My heart races swiftly
The night becomes sunny
Then it goes gloomy
For I have lost you
But how could I lose you?
For I never had you
Except on the airwaves
Captured on cable
Put onto video
But it is never enough
The more of you there is

The more video I must get
For it is never enough
For I must keep on
I am unable to stop
Every time I see you I flip, I flip
For it is an addiction
That plays over and over

Henrietta, Henrietta
I lust, I lust
For your beautiful hips drive my thrust
Henrietta, Henrietta

16

Help Help Help Help

The Drowning on the "Matt Houston" Show

One night in February I walked the streets for hours obsessed and miserable. I felt lost. My heart was racing. I smelled something burning, and I had butterflies in my stomach as if I had been punched in the gut. I went to a police station and tried to tell the officer that I needed help. I wanted to go to the mental ward and be locked up. I knew there was something wrong with me but I didn't know yet what it was. I thought I was insane.

The officer asked me if I had been seeing a counselor. When I told him who my counselor was, he seemed to recognize the name. He offered me a ride to the hospital, but I said that I could drive out myself later. I was afraid to be taken out there by the police. He told me to return to the station if I could not talk to someone at the hospital, and he would find someone for me. I said, "Okay" and left. I walked back home crying because I knew I had missed the drowning of a girl on the "Matt Houston" show. I kept telling myself that I should have watched it, I should have taped it.

At home, my mother sat at the kitchen table wondering what was wrong with me. She was in her nightgown ready to go to bed. But she waited up for me instead. I decided I was going to tell her right out what was wrong with me. "Mother, I put a pair of dance tights or pantyhose around my neck and choke myself for an orgasm!" At last the words were out. My mother's first reaction was silence when I told her what I was doing, and that I could not stop. She went to bed shortly afterward saying little. She did not understand. Now she does not even remember my telling her.

After my mother went to bed, I called the hospital and told them everything that had happened. I had called out there earlier when I found out that I had missed "Matt Houston" on television. The nurse was tired of my begging for mercy and help. Every time I called, she simply reported me to my counselor. Finally she gave the phone to a male orderly and he listened to me. All he could say was that he didn't know what to do. He kept telling me to talk to my counselor. Of course my counselor had heard all this before again and again. He just did not believe me.

I drove out to the hospital after I told the orderly I was coming. I could not get in the front door because it was locked. But the back door was open, and there were security guards there waiting impatiently to lock up the building for the night so that they could go to the nearest tavern. The orderly was expecting me. He let me in and again I told him everything. We sat on a couch in a waiting room. I insisted on staying the night there and getting a shot of something to knock me out. He kept saying that he wasn't a doctor or a nurse, so he didn't have the authorization for it. He went up to the fifth floor to tell the female head nurse what I had told him.

He returned and told me that she was unable to do anything for me. He then tried to talk me into being calm. I was breathing heavily, and all I could see was images of beautiful drowning girls in my head. The two security men paced back and forth, waiting for me either to stay or get out, so they could leave too. I wound up getting talked into making a promise to the orderly that I would not bring harm to myself or others. He stood there by the door as it was being locked and watched me drive away. I could see his face looking through the square window of the back door. I didn't sleep at all that night.

The next time I saw my counselor he told me that a policeman had called him at 6 A.M. awakening him from a sound sleep. Later the head nurse also called him from the hospital and accused me of intentionally scaring the nurses by telling them dirty stories over the phone. I found myself no closer to getting help than I had years before. I tried to buy a gun to go on a shooting spree but the forty-eight-hour waiting period stopped me. I told my counselor about this. Then he referred me to a psychiatrist in the same building. He said that I didn't need any medication.

The second psychiatrist had me take another MMPI and IQ test, word tests and puzzles. My IQ turned out to be 96. The counselor said that I was better educated than 50 percent of the nation's population. The MMPI said that I was unintentionally making myself look sick.

The first psychiatrist wanted me to bring my parents in to talk to them because he believed they had known what I was doing with the dance tights. He did not listen when I told him that they had not known, and that I had never been caught. In the end I was sent for an evaluation for one week to the university hospital in another county. There I repeated myself a thousand times to medical students, interns, and several psychiatrists. One said I was trying to shock; one said that I had to get away from my parents who were a bad influence on me; and the third, the one in charge of my case, concluded: "Patient has an obsessive compulsive personality disorder and/or an adjustment disorder of young adulthood." The report went on to say, "Willing to change. Prognosis Good." The treatment? "Move out, live on welfare, and learn independent and appropriate social skills."

I got no help at all from the fifteen professionals I had seen in three counties. It was all at the expense of the state and county. It had better be. I did not have enough money to make a down payment on all this running around and talking myself to death. I even tried a sex therapist for free. It did not work. I stopped seeing the counselor because I refused the welfare offer.

The Newspaper Trail

I was already planning suicide when, completely by accident, I made a crucial discovery about why I was the way I was. I was reading my hometown newspaper when I happened upon an article about others who had finally found peace in accidental death from the same illness as mine. It even named the coroner and the families who had dealt with this curse. The families lost their sons in autoerotic fatalities. This was the first time I had heard this term. It sounded just like my problem. Young men had hanged themselves for a sexual high and died accidentally during the act. They had probably been doing this practice for years. Some would be found with no clothes, while others were dressed in women's clothing. "Wow!" I knew what that feeling was, the strange mixture of euphoria and dread that came over me before strangling myself. It is like a seizure.

The article recounted the story of a mother and father who found their son dead in his room. He was hanging in his underwear and his feet were trussed with nylon stockings. Two other parents who experienced a similar tragedy wanted to warn others about this problem. The four of them hoped to form a support group. The article reported that according to the FBI over a thousand Americans die every year due to these autoerotic acts. These deaths are often written off as homicides or suicides. Many parents want it that way so that no one will know that their sons had a sexual disorder. People would snicker and make fun, and the word that would inevitably come up is "perversion."

Very few people understand this weird syndrome, but the coroner had some knowledge, and he recognized that it wasn't homicide or suicide. It was an accidental autoerotic fatality from asphyxiophilia, which is an illness! Finally, I had a lead, and I followed it for help.

I moved out of state to go back to school, hoping to straighten my life out. I called the coroner who knew what the boy died of, and he gave me the phone number of the reporter who wrote the article. The reporter gave me the family's phone number. The dead boy's mother had spoken with John Money, a sexologist at the Johns Hopkins University in Baltimore. She gave me his phone number. It was over the phone that I was to get the first real treatment—from a sexologist who lived a thousand miles away.

When I got in contact with Dr. Money by phone, I broke down and told him everything. He was the first person who really understood what I was talking about. I also called the other mother mentioned in the newspaper who had lost her son; she, too, gave me support in dealing with my problem. What a tragedy that both mothers lost their sons. The same fate was awaiting me, I'm sure. They helped me in a way no one else could have. They believed me, they knew, they saw, they went through it. If the article had not been written about them, and I hadn't gotten into contact with Dr. Money, I would be dead by now.

Dr. Money did not use the MMPI like the counselors I had been seeing before, who gave it to me every time I wanted help. He did not give me a bunch of stupid ink blot tests, puzzles to do, blocks to put together, or IQ tests. All these tests were given to me numerous times, and they failed every time. I write to Dr. Money all the time, and we talk weekly by phone. He has authorized medication for me.

Depo-Provera

I get one shot every seven days from an M.D. who is a surgeon in urology. He's not a mental health professional but a specialist in problems of the sex organs. He understood my problem and he got in contact with Dr. Money. He didn't laugh at me when I told him. He believed me and expressed concern. He was very serious and did what professionals are supposed to do— help people.

My curse has been put under control. I still have head-rush attacks, but now they strike several months apart. They are similar to the seizures that I had before, but they no longer lead to self-strangulation. I get butterflies in my stomach, feel pressure on my temples, hear noises in my head, see the things on the walls, break out in a sweat, get that slight shakiness in my hands, and breathe heavily. I rarely smell anything burning. When I do, the sensation is very weak. The difference now is that I just have to sit down and wait until it goes away. It feels as if something in me is draining energy from me. I get kind of dizzy, and it is scary at first, but then it just runs its course and about five minutes later it wears off. It is really weird. The sexual part of it is not there any more. Just these feelings. I have somehow been dissociated from self-strangulation. That's because of the injections of Depo-Provera medication.

Since I have learned more about what sex is supposed to be, my masturbation fantasies have become conflicted, as if a great battle were taking place between what I used to think and what I now know. What I mean is that I follow through the masturbation fantasy the way I always have, with the same suspense and detail as before. But when the fantasy reaches the point where the woman used to be strangled, drowned, stabbed, shot, suffocated, or asphyxiated, something happens and she doesn't get killed. It's as if the projector jammed the film and I get a freeze on the image. Then the pleasurable orgasm comes in. I count the contractions of the orgasm while staring at the beautiful body of the girl, and then the climax is finished. That is the end of it. She doesn't get murdered.

Sometimes when I come to the part where she is supposed to die, something happens and I end up on top of her pumping up and down as if I were copulating. When the climax is over, she is still alive. But then at other times, the girl or whoever it is this time in the fantasy is murdered. But the fantasy no longer comes easily. It becomes blurred when she is supposed to be choking or drowning, and then I might get a flash of normal sexual intercourse, then flashes of the strangling or drowning again. I can't focus on one or the other. Sometimes it is no problem at all to have a masturbation murder or at other times to have a regular sex fantasy with no murder and no flashes back and forth.

I now have fantasies of me making love to a girl whom I'm in love with. I hug my pillow at night. I make love to it. Before the shots I was masturbating six times per day. Now, with the shots, it averages six times per week. I am beginning to straighten my life out, because of the two mothers who cared enough to learn about the illness that killed their sons and almost killed me, and Dr. Money whose knowledge and caring have sustained me. There is no humiliation any more.

17

Poems of Release

Water Angel: The Reincarnation

She has become the angel of the sea
With the fishes I see
In the dreams of me
She has died
Many many a time
Only to be there
All over one more time
Her image has appeared
In many shows and films
Many girls I have known
Have taken her form
Each one happening
One after another
And each time
I fly into a fugue
One after another
For she has died
Many times on the screen
In many murders featured
In many of these scenes
Other people are entertained
Terrified, thrilled, bored
But I freak out
And fly into the fugue
For it is Water Angel again
Drowning over and over
Causing agony for me

For years I never knew why
I have come close to dying too
And I never knew why
Nor could I stop
But the day has come
For the explanation of myself
The Asphyxiophiliac Syndrome
That has cursed me
And the man who invented
A cure for me
Who has spent
His entire life
In research
Into syndromes like mine
The sexologist of our time
And after this time
And into the next
For he has become
The center of all things
The reason for the explanation of things
Things about myself
That I didn't understand
But I do now
Because of him
For he has cared
With the philosophy of
"It's me and you against the syndrome"
He didn't ask dumb questions like the other doctors asked
He has the brain
Which has helped me piece together
The most mind boggling puzzle
My own brain
And the tricks it has played on me
Thus Depo-Provera
Has been the medication for me
And it has to be
For it is the only medicine
That has changed things for me
And that is the treatment
That should be used around the nation
And the world
But it is not

Because most professionals
And other people too
Have one great prejudice
They are paraphilically blind

My lovemap of Water Angel
Is still there
If only I could have one
Who is like her
But I am afraid of loving a girl
Some kind of fear
As if she might leave me
For someone else
And thus the memory of Water Angel
Is clear to me now
When she wore blue jeans
And a white blouse
That wasn't tucked in
Her eyes were brown
Her hair was brown
It was long and curly
And thrown in a pony tail
In the back of her head
And it bounced as she walked
She had the most beautiful scream
Just like the beautiful screams
In the movies and TV shows
And it is a clear memory now
Whereas before
She vanished from me
From my conscious memory
A total blankness of her
As if she didn't exist
I just had some dreams
And nightmares too
The headaches and the nosebleeds
That mystified all who knew
I couldn't remember her
But somehow
I didn't forget

I Love the Night

I love the night
I love the thunder
And I love the lightning
The night is exciting
It gives me a head rush
A rush of endorphins
Which wreaks havoc in my brain
The thunder gives me a feeling of great power
The lightning gives me energy
I feel part of the lightning
As if it were talking to me
Then the thunder is the aftermath
Of each flash of lightning
And then I get that nice head rush
The feeling of great power
That excites me

I want to make love
When it is thundering and lightning
I want to make love all through the stormy night
Lying in bed
Hopping up and down
Bobbing up and bobbing down
The lightning flashes
It gives me more energy
I fall in love with her more
Then the thunder
And I am sloshing inside of her
She is wild
Rubbing my chest
Playing with my body
Kissing me and holding me
Grabbing it and letting it go
As it sloshes around inside of her
Flopping in and out
Driving her crazy
Driving me mad
I love her
I love her
She's mine she's mine

I would die for her
I'd die loving her
I feel like I am part of her
I wish she was part of me
That our blood flowed the same
I feel like she and I were Thunder and Lightning
Making love with each other
Like the Thunder and Lightning
Me as the Thunder
And she as the Lightning
I loved that Night

I Belong To Space

Space is one big black ocean
Space is a place for adventure
Space can bend time
Space can kill
Space can terrify
Space can do all of these things to living beings like us
However, space is a place for love too
Space is peaceful
Space is beautiful
Space possesses millions and billions and trillions of paintings
Whose paintings?
Who painted them?
Who is the artist?
Who lived long enough to paint all the artworks of space?
Maybe this artist has no life span at all
Maybe he or she or it or what is space itself
Maybe space is the artist
For space is everywhere
So space must be the guilty one
For space can do anything
And space can do nothing
It does as it pleases
Maybe space is alive
Maybe it has a conscience
It thinks
It talks
It communicates

It can foretell the future
It can record the past
It lives in the present and it will live in the future
It lived in the past and maybe before that
For space is confusing and endless
Space can be a tomb or maybe space could be a paradise
If there were only a ship that could take me to the stars
A ship that traveled beyond the speed of light
Imagine a spaceship that could prove Einstein wrong
A ship that could smash the light year and crush the time traps
A ship that could reach the inner secret of space
Find out why it is endless or maybe it isn't
Maybe one could actually speak to space and learn its language
Maybe it knows all the languages and it can speak to us in ours
I look up in the sky and feel like a part of space
I feel like I belong to it
When I look up at the stars and see how they are scattered across
I feel like I am floating and floating and floating
For space is a place for adventure
Or it can bend time, kill and terrify
For I have imagined an alien on another planet looking at earth
Wondering at the earth that looks like a blue star
And wondering if
There is anyone on it
Yes, yes, yes there is
I'm on it
I'm on the blue star
I'm part of space whatever it is
I'm part of it
I belong to it
I am space

18

I Will Not Drown

Solid Ground

Last night I had a number of dreams that were so vivid it seemed as if they were really happening. In the one I remember most, I was alone hiking on nature trails surrounded by meadows, green grass, and trees. I could see a stream in the distance. The whole scene was beautiful. This was a new place for me as I didn't recognize it from any pictures or movies, and I knew I had never been there before. It was a warm, clear day, and I stood under a blue sky.

I walked onto a wet grassy area by the stream and began to sink into it. As I sank into the ground I grabbed hold of a ledge and hung there. Behind me I saw at least an acre of land crumble and drop into the stream, which had become a raging river. I knew if I let go, then I would fall and be sucked into the undertow of the river. I had to pull myself onto solid ground. With some struggle I grasped the ledge and pulled. I saved myself. When I turned and looked, I saw all the land below me, but now it was all new: river, meadows, trails, grass, and trees. I had become as big as King Kong, and I was safe. Then I woke up and wondered why my brain is so complicated.

Why was trying to get treatment so wrong? Why is it so difficult for people cursed by paraphilia to get lithium, Depo-Provera, or sleeping pills? Why does the medical and psychiatric world refuse help? This thing, this disease, can and does happen.

Being listened to and having medication helped me. I get the shots I need from a local doctor who was willing to give them to me. All other therapy has taken place on the telephone with Dr. Money. Even though I was unable to fly out to meet him in person, I don't think I really need to. I have a will of my own. I am able.

Part Four

Commentary

19

The Failure of the System

To speak out and to be heard is the core of the therapeutic process. Yet this is more problematic than it might seem for many children who seek service. A professional's ability to listen is directly proportional to the respect held for those seeking assistance. The young often have a difficult time getting their voices heard by those older and wiser. Their concerns are misconstrued because of their youth and immaturity. The idea that children will "grow out of" problems is a reflection of society's wish to put these problems on a back burner where one need not take them seriously. By implication, time alone is all the therapy they need. Thus sexual problems are neglected. Neglect is a form of nosocomial abuse and malpractice. The issue of children's sexuality is controversial. Controversy over sex education and condom machines in high schools demonstrates that large sections of society misconstrue children as holy innocents, and sex as sin. The doctrines of the sinfulness of sexuality and the sexual innocence of childhood combine to warp societal and professional views of sexological therapy for children.

When children present problems, professionals label them in such a way that they are within the child and are not symptomatic of family or societal dysfunction. Placing the problem within the child requires no introspection on the part of those responsible for the functioning of any system that ostensibly serves the child. The system is always right! This allows professionals to escape from dealing openly and honestly with sexual problems among children.

Within the community at large, the paraphilias come under the purview of biomedical healing and science and the criminal justice system. The latter targets only those paraphilias which are, under the law, decreed to be criminal offenses. Officers of the criminal justice system are, according to the adversarial system of the law, adversaries of the paraphilic sex offender. It is their obligation to assume that he bears personal responsibility for his offense, and that it was completely under the control of his free will and voluntary choice. It is their obligation to assume also that the inescapable consequence of being declared guilty is punishment.

Members of the healing profession are, according to the tradition of Hippocrates, obliged to establish a doctor-patient relationship that is not adversarial. In the treatment of behavioral disorders, however, reward-and-punishment training has always exercised an insidious influence, as it does also in the training of children. Under the aegis of behavior-modification theory, punishment training is again in vogue among victimologists for the treatment of perpetrators. Victimology has blurred the dividing lines between Hippocrates, the healer, and Hammurabi, the lawgiver, in the treatment of paraphilias defined as abusive. Health-care providers are in many instances cast by law into the position of operating as undercover police informers. There are some paraphiles who, should they seek help, must be reported to the police for investigation and punishment. Only after they are in custody, or under supervision, are they permitted to receive treatment which, more often than not, is an additional quota of reward-and-punishment training. For the prevention of relapse or recidivism among paraphilic sex offenders, the efficacy of reward-and-punishment training is as questionable as it is for the prevention of epileptic seizures.

Nelson's wrathful indignation at the failure of the system set up ostensibly to help him, and those like him, needs to be heard. Here is a young man who sought help and received only a mishmash of diagnostic labels, from retardation to emotional disturbance. With every label, his chance of effective help dwindled. No one heard his voice or understood the importance of his words. Even his rage and resentment were seen as evidence that he was a retarded, emotionally disturbed attention-seeker from a dysfunctional family. None of the labelling reflected any understanding of his primary difficulty. Combine sexual problems with youth and you get professional blame or denial.

As a child becomes more and more problematic, he is fitted into more and more diagnostic categories. The complexity of the person is seen only in its fragmentation into a series of clinical categories. It is not seen as requiring a complex service delivery. Instead, a simplistic approach is deemed suitable. Nelson's would-be assistance came from the behavior modificationist camp. Time-out and other forms of punishment were used ostensibly to assist him in controlling his symptomatic behavior. Yet, as he himself so eloquently conveys, this behavior was closely linked to the growth of sexual obsession from a very early age. With the knowledge of hindsight, it is embarrassingly obvious that the use of techniques of behavior control was foolish.

Many behaviorists now interpret all behavior as a means of communication. Taken literally, this means that all attempts to stifle behavior without a conceptual understanding of its nature and idiosyncratic intent, not only binds, but also effectively gags a client. The relationship between inner meaning and observable behavior must be taken seriously. While it is recognized that inner meanings have a role in human behavior and interaction for the rich, white, and able, it is more difficult to see this for the young, disabled, and poor. Therapists must be on guard for inherent prejudices within their trade.

By everyone concerned, responsibility was placed on Nelson's young shoulders to control that which was eventually to control him. He was expected to win an internal battle that would enable him to control himself. Only then would he have earned acceptance from those in power in the school, the clinic, and his family. Despite defeats, he fought the battle well. The losses were in the persistence of imagery in dreams and masturbation fantasies, contained within themselves and not translated into action.

Reading the ever-growing detail and violence of the sexual imagery, one cannot but be in awe of the fact that no one was ever hurt. In consequence, one is obliged to recognize that a person with a paraphilia is not a willful deviant who directs and controls his sexuality into criminal or deviant acts. Nelson has acted as a responsible citizen, not as a stereotype of the sexual deviant. Without therapeutic intervention, he himself designed a program of satiation to deal with obsession sparked by television programs. Satiation is a commonly used method in behavior-modification therapy.

His yearning for treatment was evident in his search for help. He did not give up the search, even while the obsession grew both in power and in violence. The search ended only by accident, when he came across a newspaper article in which he recognized his own condition and began a series of telephone calls that led to a new form of treatment from which, for the first time, he obtained a beneficial effect. Since then, he has carried the responsibility of finding ways to meet the substantial costs of that part of his treatment which is not subsidized. He labors steadfastly at a menial job which holds no promise of fulfilling his ambitions as a film maker.

That someone like Nelson, afflicted with incessant dreams of serious acts of sexual murder, had to search tirelessly for help is societally inexcusable. When multiple murder or an act of sexual violence or autoerotic death is reported in the news, the response of some professionals is that the potentiality for such a tragedy should have been discovered earlier. Nelson's experience makes this response a mockery, for it requires that a patient must first make a self-diagnosis and then search an appropriate specialist with training in sexology. This is too much to ask of someone overwhelmed by a powerful obsession.

Treatment for Nelson was simultaneously both simple and complex. It began the day he saw the article in the newspaper. In his writings one can sense the excitement, even now, that he had upon finding a term for his predicament. From that day onward, the thing that plagued him had a name. There is great comfort in being able to identify one's tormentor, and that day Nelson realized that he was dealing with an illness, not a wickedness of sin. He also realized that others were victims of the same illness. He was not alone in the world. His response was not to repudiate his illness, but to seek improvement. For the first time he talked with a caring professional who did not label and pass judgment, but offered treatment instead. He was able at last to be heard. For the first time, his youth, his various labels, and the sexual nature of his obsessions did not lead to his being despised or rejected. In addition he had the promise of a medication, a hormone, that would enable his fantasies to be brought under control. No longer was he to be a victim.

20

Pornography and Paraphilic Imagery

For those who lack an understanding of the nature of paraphilic obsession and compulsion, the issue of maintaining control seems a simple one. The idea of being out of control of one's fantasy life seems somewhat poetic. Yet an uncontrollable fantasy, like an uncontrollable night terror or nightmare, dominates and rules. Nelson became a victim of very powerful images, with an autonomy of their own. Even the preview of a television show in which a brown-haired girl was seen being drowned or strangled would be enough to send him into a paraphilic trance from which he would escape only when the fantasy itself had subsided.

Television scenes of drowning or strangling, shown on prime-time, network television for family entertainment, are not obscene or pornographic, according to the Supreme Court's criteria. Yet Nelson himself recognized that, for him, they were the equivalent of regular commercial pornography of the type that is prohibited on network television, and that he personally found so disgusting that he avoided it. "The Meese Commission on Pornography missed something," he wrote in an angry critique. "They missed the drownings of girls on network television. Whenever I see a drowning or strangling, I go crazy. I can go up to a maximum of six orgasms in one day, over a period of several days, and it can be all wound up around seeing a girl drown on television."

He was referring to a particular episode of the "Matlock" series to which he had had a devastatingly difficult and desperate reaction. He explained it in a letter, as follows.

I haven't slept in 120 hours. I sat in front of the television and started to masturbate at 6:15 even though the show did not start until 7:00. I wanted to time the orgasm to happen during the scene where the girl gets drowned. The murder of course was a long one. Drownings are the longest murders on television. It takes longer for a person to drown than it does to die from a shooting or a stabbing. I'm talking about normal prime time. Most of the shows that I go insane over I've seen on network television.

I found that the whole sixty minutes went very fast and I was completely engrossed and disgustingly entertained by all of it. If I had seen it in color, then I would have seen the blueness of color in the water mixed with the surging white caps; and the flesh color of her soft beautiful skin I would have seen when she was held under. My heart beat was 120 per minute. I took three times as much of the pills that the doctor gave me.

I wonder what it would be like to drown someone? I wonder what it would feel like if I was a killer? I wonder what it feels like to be held under with water sloshing around and coming into your lungs? You would choke on the water. You would struggle. You would get dizzy from the lack of air. You would die. But the worst of it is over, except for the sad fact that I failed, again.

The turmoil triggered by "Matlock" was horrendous and totally disruptive for over a week, from the first advertising preview until days after the actual program. Nelson described his desperation to a professional friend who had volunteered to help, where possible. The professional's advice had been couched in terms of redirecting one's own imagery and responses. In his reply, Nelson wrote as follows:

I thought that your suggestions were nice ones, but I have heard them before. I would like to explain to you that I did not choose to watch the drowning of the girl in the hot tub on "Matlock." I DO NOT CHOOSE to watch these things. It may seem like choosing but that isn't the case. I was pushed into it. Yes, it was a trap, but not one that I put myself into. It just happened that way. I have no choice! You mentioned about staying away from these programs and watching something else. Well when this kind of thing is on it is a terrible and horrible, agonizing and torturing thing not to watch it. And it is the same for watching it. It is terrible and horrible and agonizing to watch it. There is no escape either way. I suppose it sounds like I watch a lot of television, but in fact I watch less and less every day. But when I see an accidental flash of a commercial advertising a girl getting drowned on the show, that is the end of it for the word "control." There is no control of any kind at all. I have fought this thing, this entity, a hunger that does not die. It tells me what to do. I cannot tell it anything. From the moment that I saw that excerpt of what the murder was going to be, that image became trapped in my brain and played over and over, and over and over again and again for days and days. And it makes me mad that I can't get other people to understand that the woman looked like she got an orgasm when she was drowned, and that the killer got a turn on when he drowned her in the hot tub. All of the suspects in the show looked like they all would have liked to drown her. They all looked like they were getting a turn on from her drowning. Even Matlock himself (played by Andy Griffith) got a turn on and enjoyed the fact that she drowned. And he was turning himself on when he had the real killer on the stand in the court room, and he had the killer nailed to the wall when he explained how he drowned her. Matlock said it like this, "When you drowned that poor girl . . . " And he also said, "And that's when you closed your hands around her neck and held her head under the water." You see, Matlock figured out how he was the killer by the fact that the killer's watch had stopped one minute after he drowned her because water got in the watch. I mean you can see that they all got a turn on to it. A child could see it, damn it!

Usually there are very few 30 second long drowning murders on television that are brand new. Thirty seconds is a long time to see a girl in a black bikini, or a red one for that matter, drowning on television. When there is a shooting, it is just a second or two, or a stabbing (slasher films and *Psycho* don't count) is just a second or two. And this is network television. They just don't drag on murders except drownings. I wish I knew why. Do you have any idea how long it took in slow motion for the cheerleader to roll down the cement pavement into the dam in the made for television movie *With Intent to Kill?* Probably not, but it's a long time. And just count off 30 seconds on your watch and see just how long it is and try to think how many camera angles and shots can happen in a drowning of a girl. And drownings are more expensive to shoot for a movie or a show and it takes longer to film and edit a drowning murder too. I wish I could direct a show with a drowning in it. I did not learn to eroticize death and sex fantasies. They just flew into my brain, and that was when I was little, and the reason is because I got no sex education, and when I saw kissing on television or movies it made me sick to look at it. So I really did not train myself. I was taught by other forces beyond my control.

I have learned new erotic values already, but it is very hard to get them into focus in my brain and to fantasize and masturbate to them. I know you know that. I have tried them and they do happen, but only when they want to. It's weird how it happens. I will be lying there masturbating myself, and when it gets to the lusting, pleasurable orgasm the intercourse fantasy pops in. And there it is! She will be hugging me and I will be hugging and kissing her and we are both thrusting into each other. That's what you said was going to happen when you wrote to me last year. You said it about when I was making love to my pillow, when I pretend it's a girl, and you said that a good orgasmic fantasy will pop in. I still love my pillow, and I pretend that she loves me and is touching me and rubbing my chest, and we talk to each other and everything. But when a drowning is on television, that's it, that's the end. I go crazy and I am obsessed and there is no choice. I'm in misery either way. I do pretend, though, that I am with other people too, like you suggested, and I talk to the air and I talk to the walls though I think that there is somebody there that I can only see. Anyone spotting me would think I was crazy and think that I was really talking to the wall.

I don't reward myself with an orgasm after re-enforcing the fantasy. The orgasm is the only way that I can get rid of the madness that possessed me. The fantasy may come in a dream, or a nightmare, and when I wake up in the middle of the night my penis is sitting there, hard as rock, and it feels two feet long, and if I do not masturbate I toss and turn all night in agony, and I will fly into another nightmare that is identical in content, and then wake up again. It will be just 20 minutes after the first nightmare, and my penis simply will not go soft until I get the orgasm and get rid of the fantasy, so then I can go back to sleep. My penis does not obey the laws of medicine, it will not go soft by itself until I give it the orgasm. Oh sometimes it will go soft on its own. But sometimes it will not. I have learned to crawl. I have been crawling for years. But when something like this flashes on the screen, that is it; I have no choice.

It's like other things that happen to me when I am asleep. Like I have bitten my tongue in my sleep and I have woken up with it sore. And I also bite my cheek. Sometimes I jerk and twitch while I am asleep. People have seen me sleep and told me. That is what it is like when I freak out over a girl drowning in the hot tub and she gets an orgasm. I was under control of myself until one night before the show. But then I lost it. Something hit me and that was it. No escape!

In this letter, there is not actual use of the phrases "altered state of consciousness," or "paraphilic fugue state." (Latin *fugere* means "to fly.") Having his own everyday state of consciousness take leave, and "fly away," is, however, precisely what the words of the letter do, in their own way, convey. Having this daily consciousness "fly away" is what happens to ordinary people every time they go to sleep, and they think nothing of it. To have a similar thing happen while wide awake is altogether different. It is more like having an epileptic attack of the type classified as a temporal-lobe or psychomotor seizure, which occurs without convulsions and with an alteration, but not a total loss of consciousness.

In Nelson's experience, there has been, ever since puberty, another type of epileptic-like attack which he so much took for granted that he had been in treatment for four years before it was mentioned. He first knew about it at age twelve from another boy at school who demonstrated what had just happened: with clenched fists, arms extended downwards, and closed eyes, Nelson had a shaking spell. He had not realized it was happening, but he thought he may have had some sort of brief vision. On future occasions, when a similar thing occurred, he would bite the index finger of his right hand. These many years later, his finger bears a large callus that does not bleed when his teeth sink into it.

Nowadays, the finger biting is accompanied by spinning clockwise, if he is in a standing position. It is also accompanied by hallucinatory visions of violently attacking people who have made his life miserable, for example, at work.

An attack may also occur while he is lying in bed listening to music to which he is mentally composing one of the many movie scripts and scenarios that he would like to produce. His arms will be folded and elevated above his chest, and his body rocks from side to side. Then, as violent imagery displaces the imagery of the movie script, and the finger biting begins, he no longer hears the music. "I was closed off to it," he said. "Sometimes, I'll jump out of bed, spinning, and I'll start screaming for real, and yelling curses and obscenities. And if my mother comes in and asks what I'm yelling at, I'll say it's nothing."

He has taken Tegretol, on prescription, in an effort to control these seizures, but they have not completely subsided.

21

Two Letters to Professionals

Ever since beginning treatment, Nelson has been concerned about help for other paraphiles, as this book demonstrates. He has written two statements for the education of professionals. One is a letter addressed to the Western Regional Meeting of the American Association of Sex Educators, Counselors and Therapists (AASECT). The other is a follow-up to the first letter.

Letter Addressed to AASECT Meeting

The first letter gives a very accurate and complete summary of both the subjective and behavioral manifestations of asphyxiophilia. It is addressed to:

Dear Members of the Association,
   To be at the mercy of a paraphilia is like being a slave to lust and ecstasy. It commands me. I have no will of my own when my paraphilia takes over. It usually takes over without warning, and once it starts, it must finish all the way to the end of its course. Like a virus taking its course. Like a tornado storm taking its course. Swift like the tornado, destructive in accuracy like the zig zag of the funnel cloud. My temples pound like the thunder putting pressure on them. Then when the oxygen to my brain is cut off, I hear a mass of head noises intensifying like hail falling from the sky and smashing onto a Fiberglas roof. Tingling sensations of incredible ecstasy tickle through my sex organ. It starts to swell in beautiful hardness through my nylon bikini underwear while the nylon leotard of a beautiful woman tightens, tighter and tighter around my neck, until I cannot make any more of my marvellous choking sounds.
   My windpipe is totally closed, and I cannot breathe or scream, but I try because it adds to the fantastic excitement to see my stomach suck in and out with no air coming in. And it's marvellous to see my lungs go up and down trying to suck in air, but nothing comes in. My saliva or

the spit in my mouth is building like mad, and I try to swallow it, and it's fascinating to swallow, but the spit doesn't go anywhere. It just bounces back into my mouth, and then I try to force it down, but it still won't go down. Then more spit builds up in my mouth, and the whole time I'm watching my body's reactions to all of this in front of the mirror, while at the same time I'm struggling and strangling and fighting my attacker, who is also homosexual like me, but in the paraphilic fantasy attack only. Then when I cannot take it any more I release the women's leotard and my windpipe opens once again.

Then I fall to the floor, and I masturbate with my fingers on my genitals, and have in mind a beautiful girl getting strangled or drowned to death. Her last choke is at the great point of orgasm, and then the milky white stuff squirts out, and I get great relief, as if a ton of rocks was just lifted off my back. The sticky stuff is all over my chest and some on my one arm. I don't wipe it off. I let it stay there and get hard when it dries. Then I'm exhausted and tired and weak, and I want to sleep, but I don't sleep because then I'm terrified. I say to myself, "Why did I do this? I told myself I would never do it again." I keep telling myself this. I have been telling myself this for the past two years, even though I started over six years ago, but it was not this severe. It grew as time went on, and it gets worse as I get older. I've been saying to myself all this time that I won't do it. I won't do it. But I did it anyway.

Lots of times I smell something burning before I go out of control. Then I have some head noises starting, and my fingers tremble a little. Then I start to breathe quicker, and I get butterflies in my stomach. Then the great rush begins. Oh, I was recognizing the warning signs in time, but I had no one to go to. Anyone I did go to, numerous psychiatrists and psychologists, lectured me not to call up the hotlines for mental health, freaking out the nurses and nurses' aides answering the phones. They didn't believe me.

The MMPI didn't believe me, and it was given to me twice. The second one was worse than the first because it said I was faking. For a year and a half I was bounced from one testing to a master evaluation in the psycho ward at a very acclaimed hospital in another city, in which the whole thing I was talking about got turned into a battle against my parents, who knew nothing about my problem.

I did not learn my strangling of myself from anybody, nor did I learn it from pornography books, nor from magazines, or rock videos. But from prime-time TV. When I see a woman with a tight swimsuit on "Matt Houston" get pulled underwater while she's swimming, and then she is held there by a killer in scuba gear, I go into a paraphiliac attack. When I see a woman in a scanty bikini on "Charlie's Angels" getting drowned, I lose control. These shows are on normal TV. When the beautiful girl on the TV movie, "With Intent to Kill," slips and rolls over and over and over down the concrete slanted pavement into the rushing-water of the dam, in slow motion, and she's wearing a white high-school cheerleader's uniform, I can think of nothing but the tight bikini underwear under the dress skirt of the uniform. I go out of control and masturbate, playing the death or murder over and over and over in my mind, masturbating six times throughout the same night, right after seeing it, unless I can save myself by video taping it when I see it. Then I can play the VCR tape over and over and over again watching it on the TV screen all the time until I get tired of it. Only in this way will my mind stop playing it over and over and over so much. I get sad and bawl and cry like a two-year-old if I don't get to tape it and play it over and over again.

Then I may get into my leotard and bikini underwear and choke myself in front of the mirror right after I dress up, and pretend that I have sexual relations with another homosexual before he takes my leotard off me and strangles me to death with it. Then I masturbate with my penis afterward.

I don't look at porno magazines because I cannot stand to see the ugly hairy beasts with their ugly, hairy, slimy penises having sex with those beautiful women. But I like the lesbian porno magazines because that looks cleaner. The only man's butt and penis I like is my own, in front of the mirror, in my paraphiliac attack, covered in 100 percent stretch nylon.

So there you have it, absurd, bizarre, weird, perverted, whatever it's being called by people who don't understand my problem of being at the mercy of a paraphilia. My mind never rests even in my sleep. I dream of women drowning by somebody pulling them under, or I dream of jumping in front of the mirror to strangle myself for my superb pleasure of lust and ecstasy, which runs and is practically ruining my life.

Sincerely,

The Asphyxiophiliac Still Living

Letter Addressed to the Regional Secretary of AASECT

This letter, unsolicited, is the reply to a note from the regional secretary, thanking Nelson for the foregoing letter to AASECT members. It is addressed to:

Dear Bob,

It has been a long time since I received your letter of January 4th, so I thought I would write back.

In your last letter you asked me precisely how much help I am getting on the Depo-Provera program.

I have not strangled myself for over a year because, of course, of the Depo-Provera. My dosage started at 500mg every 7 days. However, I did have some trouble a couple of months ago and so then my injection went up to 600mg every 7 days. I have remained unstrangled still since then.

Before I was on Depo-Provera I could masturbate up to 6 times a day and, in rare cases, 12 times in one day, like on one very nightmarish lusting obsessive day when I was 17. But now that I am on the shots, I masturbate an average of once a day and sometimes twice a day.

When the orgasm comes I get sticky goop, but it is not white like semen is; it is clear.

The fantasies have been changing also, I assume, from the psychotherapy sessions I have been getting from Dr. Money. I have been told by him the ways that people have sex and that women like to have sex too. He has been giving me a sex educational course of sorts which has fed into my brain, and my lovemap seems to be straightening out and becoming more normalized as the weeks go by.

For example: Where I used to strangle myself, now I sleep with an extra pillow and I pretend that it is a girl and that we have a super-duper-fun sexual relationship. I actually pretend that I am trying to make love to the pillow, but my imagination shows a girl in its place. I sleep with the pillow and talk to it as if it were her. I am really practising for when I really get to make love to somebody someday. I actually hold the pillow as if it were her when we go to sleep with my arms around her and everything. I imagine her face, hair, eyes, which are usually brown hair and brown eyes, and I imagine her beautiful nakedness too.

My masturbation fantasies, on the other hand, seem to be confused from time to time. Usually when I had a fantasy while masturbating, the girl would either be strangled, drowned, or suffocated in some way. In others I was a homosexual getting strangled or drowned or suffocated in some way. This was before I was on the Depo-Provera shots.

Now, after being on the shots, my fantasy starts out to be a murder, but at the end, the mental imagery stops and then I just think about the feeling of the orgasm, and the murder fantasy never does carry through. In other fantasies, when the murder is carried out, it is a girl (Jodie Foster) who is the killer and she kills a girl with brown hair and eyes. (Jodie has gold blonde hair and blue eyes.)

In most of the fantasies now, one girl will be in the fantasy and she is supposed to get killed but then my mental imagery flips over or switches over to another girl in a different setting. My mind switches as if it turned the channel on a television set to another station. So my mind might switch to another girl in a different setting, and then, when the orgasm comes, my mind imagery goes blank and I just feel the orgasm without any imagery at all.

And then again there is another where she is supposed to get killed, whoever the girl is this time. I know hundreds of girls. But when the orgasm comes, I'm on top of her and we are having intercourse and making love in the fantasy, which I never did imagine without her getting killed, until after talking to Dr. Money and taking the Depo-Provera shots.

I never am the killer in the fantasies, and I am never killed in the fantasies any more.

More and more I am having intercourse fantasies and kissing fantasies, and they happen when the orgasm comes, whereas before the girl always had to die.

There is more touching and loving and sex in the imagery of the orgasm now, and I can imagine what it could be like to penetrate the vagina, which I was never able to imagine or dream about before.

And then yet another example of my imagery is where the fantasy runs in reverse. The murder of the girl happens first during the masturbation, but long before the orgasm comes. When the orgasm comes, the girl is alive again, and she and I are having sex and love, and she wasn't harmed at all. The murder in the beginning (which was of the girl getting strangled by Jodie Foster) didn't have any erotic sexual pleasure at all. Sexual pleasure happens only in the orgasm. So when the girl was getting killed in the beginning, it may be because my mind is killing time to get to the orgasm. But then she is at the end of the fantasy with me, as if she were never killed at all.

Yours,

Nelson

22

Treatment Strategy

Only after a long period of combined antiandrogen and counseling therapy did the actresses in Nelson's asphyxiation fantasies change roles and become lovers who engaged in lovemaking and penovaginal intercourse. Previously, Nelson's imagery of intercourse was of a vagina being defiled by an abomination, the penis. It was anathema to him. Lust was incompatible with love in one and the same partner. This is a universal principle of the paraphilias. Love is romantically idealized so that, if the subject of romantic idealization invites lust, the paraphile panics. The defiling act of lust requires devious stratagems. One stratagem is atonement and sacrifice. The self-asphyxiator atones for the defilement of lust by sacrificing himself, or herself. The antipodean atonement is the sacrifice of the partner.

The person who has a paraphilia does not know how to explain himself. He is quite accurate when he claims not to know why he does what he does (and likewise the paraphilic woman). For the paraphile, the sundering of love from lust means that each belongs to a completely different state of mind, one being split off or dissociated from the other. Dissociation may occur in other contexts. In Nelson's case, it was evident in the two states of consciousness in which he wrote—one for writing business letters and daily notes, and the other resembling a trance in which he wrote down poems and literary prose, and also composed movie scripts, almost as if he were transcribing from dictation.

The two states of consciousness, one on each side of the dissociative split, may be so dramatically different from each other that one recognizes hardly any similarity between them. That is why one speaks of one of them as a paraphilic fugue state, and the other as representing a more normal mental state. In some cases the two states may differ in such a way that what happens in one state is not remembered or only dimly remembered when the change to the other state takes place. This is the phenomenon of dual or multiple personality. Paraphilic fugue state more accurately applies to Nelson's case than does dual personality, with the exception of the periods when he underwent an attack that began with finger biting. Then he was a changed person with a dramatically changed personality.

When a dual or multiple personality coexists with paraphilia, it is not uncommon to find an antecedent childhood history of a traumatizing home life, possibly with extreme neglect and abuse, and in some cases, traumatizing sexual abuse. Although Nelson catalogued many grievances against members of his family, on the whole his home life was not conspicuously traumatizing as compared with that of other neighborhood children.

Irrespective of where they came from, not all of the components that contributed to the making of asphyxiophilia may have originated in the sexual centers and pathways of Nelson's brain, but that is where they converged and formed a final common pathway. The paraphilic pattern became lodged, tenaciously, in much the same way as a native language becomes tenaciously lodged, once it has entered the brain. It could not be pried loose under the influence of talking treatment alone, without the assistance of pharmacologic intervention, namely with the hormone Depo-Provera (medroxyprogesterone acetate). Under the influence of the two treatments in combination, change began to take place.

Depo-Provera is the trade name of a synthetic hormone manufactured by Upjohn. Its generic name, medroxyprogesterone acetate, incorporates the name of the natural hormone, progesterone, for Depo-Provera is a synthetic progestinic hormone.

Progesterone is one of the three main sex hormones. The other two are testosterone and estrogen. All three are made in the testicles of male animals, and the same three are made in the ovaries of female animals.

Unlike various other hormones, progesterone, testosterone, and estrogen are classified as steroid hormones. Steroid is derived from Greek words meaning solid oil, in other words, a form of fat. The basic molecule of all three sex hormones is a fat molecule. It is, in fact, the molecule with the well known name "cholesterol." In the body's laboratory of molecules, Nature, the technician in charge, uses enzymes to change cholesterol into sex steroids. Progesterone comes off the assembly line first. It is then turned into testosterone, and testosterone is turned into estrogen.

Progesterone got its name because its blood level is highest during gestation or pregnancy, and estrogen because its blood level is highest when an animal is in estrus, or heat, and is ovulating. Although they are together referred to as female hormones, they circulate in the male's bloodstream and so do male hormones. Their difference in males and females is not absolute, but relative: in males they are present in much smaller quantities than in females. In reverse, the same applies to testosterone, the hormone named after the testicles and known also as androgen, from Greek *andros*, meaning male.

Progesterone does not linger in the male body before it is turned into testosterone. Thus the two hormones do not enter into competition with one another. Competition is intense, however, between testosterone and the synthetic progestin, Depo-Provera. In the treatment of paraphilia, Depo-Provera is injected intramuscularly and is gradually absorbed into the bloodstream over the ensuing week or so. The amount is sufficient so that the molecules of Depo-Provera jostle the molecules of testosterone aside and trick the cells that bind with testosterone into binding with themselves, instead.

The therapeutic value of this trickery hinges on the fact that the molecules of the progestinic hormone (Depo-Provera) are biologically inert as compared with the very energetic molecules of testosterone. The upshot is that cells anywhere in the body that are energized by testosterone are put at rest by Depo-Provera. Androgen-producing cells within the testicles themselves go on sabbatical, so that the blood level of testosterone, the main testicular androgen, becomes drastically reduced. In other words, Depo-Provera acts as an antiandrogen.

Subjectively, the experience of the person taking the treatment is one of increased calm and of no longer being excessively ruled by a dictatorship of erotic thoughts, imagery, and fantasy. The fantasies themselves diminish. These mental effects may be the result of a direct, erotic calming action of Depo-Provera on sex-regulating brain cells in the preoptic region, deep behind the bridge of the nose. In this part of the brain of male monkeys, it requires only fifteen minutes after an injection of radioactively labeled Depo-Provera for the labeled molecules to show up within the brain cells themselves.

The effects of treatment with Depo-Provera have been compared with those of surgical castration. The great difference is that surgical castration is for life, whereas hormonal treatment need not be. When Depo-Provera is terminated, its side effects are reversible. If there is a threat of relapse, a booster treatment can be given to prevent it.

There are other synthetic steroidal hormones that, like Depo-Provera, have an antiandrogenic effect. One of them is Androcur (cyproterone acetate). Its use for the treatment of paraphilias in Europe parallels the use of Depo-Provera in the United States, where it has not yet been cleared by the FDA (Federal Drug Administration).

Not all antiandrogens are steroidal hormones. One that is particularly effective in completely blocking the biosynthesis of androgen is the drug flutamide. It has not yet been tested for the treatment of paraphilia.

Historically, the first sexological use of Depo-Provera for the treatment of paraphilia was in 1966 at Johns Hopkins by Money in association with the endocrinologists Claude Migeon and Marco Rivarola. In the preceding decade, it had been used to suppress the precocious onset of puberty (pubertas precox) in boys and girls between the ages of one and six.

Today it is possible that a new hormone that has proved itself in the treatment of precocious puberty might also be effective for paraphilias. The new hormone, known as an LHRH analogue, is a trimmed-down molecule of Luteinizing Hormone Releasing Hormone. This is the hormone, released from actual brain cells in the hypothalamus, that instructs the pituitary gland to release luteinizing hormone. Like LHRH, LHRH analogue has a stimulating effect, if released episodically, and a suppressing effect, if released continuously. It is the latter which puts the reins on precocious puberty, and may possibly do the same for paraphilia.

Another medication, newly arrived on the horizon of treatments for paraphilia, is neither a hormone, nor an antiandrogen, but a drug to reduce anxiety. It is buspirone hydrochloride (BuSpar). Given to anxiety-ridden men who had also a paraphilic obsession, it unexpectedly reduced not only the symptoms of anxiety, but also the paraphilic obsession.

Still another unexpected discovery in recent years pertains to lithium carbonate, the drug well known for treatment of bipolar (manic-depressive) disorder. When it is prescribed for depression in patients who also have a paraphilic obsession, the response in some cases is a reduction of the depression and the paraphilic obsession. Lithium carbonate may be combined with Depo-Provera. It may also be used alone if the hormone is for some reason contraindicated. After four years on Depo-Provera, Nelson undertook a trial treatment with lithium carbonate pills, in part because the hormone injection sites on his thighs had developed an excess of scar tissue. The gains made while on the antiandrogen were not lost as his testosterone level returned to normal, but were sustained under the influence of lithium carbonate, along with slowly progressive additional improvement. The sexological talking treatment continued. No longer drowning, Nelson walked on solid ground.

www.ingramcontent.com/pod-product-compliance
Lightning Source LLC
Chambersburg PA
CBHW031534260326
41914CB00032B/1804/J